# WRITE
## YOUR OWN
# SCI-FI

**union
square
kids**

**NEW YORK**

UNION SQUARE KIDS and the distinctive Union Square
Kids logo are trademarks of Union Square & Co.

Union Square & Co., LLC, is a subsidiary of Sterling
Publishing Co., Inc.

ISBN 978-1-4549-4653-3

For information about custom editions, special sales,
and premium and corporate purchases, please contact
specialsales@unionsquareandco.com.

Manufactured in China

2 4 6 8 10 9 7 5 3 1

06/22

unionsquareandco.com

# WRITE
## YOUR OWN
# SCI-FI

### YOUR GUIDE TO WRITING FICTION
### THAT'S OUT OF THIS WORLD

PHILIP WOMACK

ILLUSTRATED BY KATY TUTTLE

union
square
kids

NEW YORK

# CONTENTS

# ABOUT THIS BOOK

## EACH CHAPTER CONTAINS A GUIDE TO THE SUB-GENRES WITHIN SCI-FI, WITH PLENTY OF PROMPTS YOU CAN USE TO HYPERDRIVE YOUR OWN WRITING. YOU'LL FIND FACTOIDS AND TERMS FROM THE SCI-FI WORLD TOO.

There are six main chapters, each concerning a particular aspect of creative writing.

Within each chapter is a sub-genre, such as Dystopias, Invasions, or Aliens!

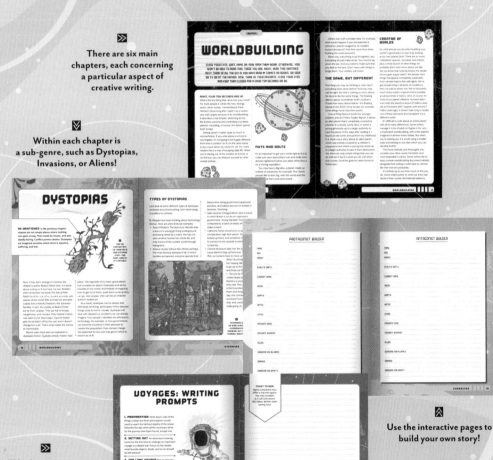

You'll find creative prompts after each sub-genre: these help you get into the groove with your writing.

Use the interactive pages to build your own story!

Use the lined pages to try out a prompt or two. There are also facts and terms on each page, to help you along the way.

# MEET PHILIP

I'VE ALWAYS DREAMED OF OTHER WORLDS. THAT SENSE OF OTHER, STRANGER LIVES, EXISTING THROUGHOUT THE UNIVERSE. WRITING ABOUT THEM IS NOT ONLY IMMENSELY ENJOYABLE, IT'S ALSO A WAY OF EXPLORING IDEAS FREELY.

## SCI-FI SKILLS

Writing science fiction (sci-fi) can be a total blast. You'll create cool plots, amazing characters, and galactic settings. You'll also design exciting battle scenes—pow! Whizz! Bash! You'll have heroes and villains, friends and enemies. But most of all, what you need to do is avoid clichés—things that have been done many times before—and make old ideas new.

## TOOLS OF THE TRADE

It may seem odd to say this in a book about sci-fi writing, but I always say you should write with a pen and paper first. Your thoughts will flow more clearly. You won't have interruptions from emails and messages, and so forth. You can then type up or dictate or whatever you want to do to get your prose on the screen. Who knows, by the time this book is published, maybe someone will have invented a direct thought transference machine. . . .

You may, of course, be nothing like me, and be quite happy typing straight onto the screen. If you do this, then I sincerely suggest you turn off your cell phone and disconnect your laptop from the Internet. Certainly switch off all the alerts that blare and beep onto your screen every two minutes. They can wait, I promise.

## THE EVER-EXPANDING UNIVERSE

The world of sci-fi is enormous, and it would be impossible to cover everything in a short book. I've chosen as many different kinds of examples here as possible. They'll help you make your own work come alive. Do you want to write about eight-legged humanoid pandas battling to save their homeworld against terrifying robots? Then keep reading! You'll also find out about things like cyberpunk, space battles, virtual reality, and utopias.

"The reason I think science fiction is the crucial literature of the 20th century is that it is the only one to put greeting the alien at its heart. And that's important because the 20th century is the one where humanity changed from inward-looking village creatures to creatures forced to encounter otherness on a global scale all the time. How well we manage that encounter, how well we can accept rather than hate and try to kill the other, will define the viability of the human future. There could hardly have been a more important topic! And it is at the heart of SF."

– Adam Roberts (*Get Started in: Writing Science Fiction and Fantasy*)

**PHILIP WOMACK** has been reading and writing about other worlds since he was a small boy. He has written eight novels for children, all of them fantastical. His most recent, *Wildlord*, centers on a battle between ancient magic and new alchemy. He taught creative writing for several years at a London university before becoming a Royal Literary Fund Fellow. He lives in London with his wife, three children, and dog, Una.

# INTRODUCTION

A VERY LONG TIME AGO, ON A PLANET JUST LIKE OURS, A YOUNG MAN FLEW TO THE MOON. THERE HE BECAME CAUGHT UP IN A GALACTIC BATTLE BETWEEN THE KING OF THE SUN AND THE KING OF THE MOON OVER THE COLONIZATION OF THE MORNING STAR (VENUS). IT INVOLVED ENORMOUS SPACE SPIDERS.

Does this storyline sound familiar? Nope, it's not the plot of the latest action-packed Marvel movie. It's from *A True Story*, which was composed by a Greek writer called Lucian, nearly 2,000 years ago. Lucian wasn't strictly writing sci-fi—in fact, he doesn't use any technology. His hero travels to the Moon in a whirlwind, not a spaceship. But his story demonstrates that we've always looked to the stars and wondered what was up there. And we've always imagined technologies that go beyond our own. In Homer's ancient epic poem, *The Iliad*, the blacksmith god Hephaestus is served by bronze maidens. Some might call those robots.

As a result of this, you could argue that science fiction has been around almost as long as storytelling. We love imagining exotic, otherworldly locations. We enjoy thinking about the future and what it might bring. Our own world makes innovations every year that once seemed impossible. Believe it or not, there was once a time when touchscreens seemed amazing.

## THE BEGINNING

The history of modern sci-fi really began with Mary Shelley's 19th-century novel *Frankenstein,* in which a young scientist named Victor Frankenstein patches together a monster from body parts. The Age of Science had begun, and nothing would ever be the same again.

Shelley looked at what was happening around her, as you should too! Read or watch the news and use it to inspire your novel. The scientist Galvini had made dead frogs' legs twitch with electricity in 1780. Shelley thought about the consequences of this. All around, the

Industrial Revolution was changing the way the world worked. She considered the immense dangers of power, as Frankenstein becomes a victim of his own creation.

Many writers then followed. Edgar Allen Poe, Nathaniel Hawthorne, and most notably, Jules Verne, who in *20,000 Leagues Under the Sea* sent Captain Nemo down into the ocean in a submarine, and in *Journey to the Center of the Earth* had explorers finding dinosaurs underground. The great H.G. Wells—who was himself a scientist—introduced us to time travel right at the end of the 19th century with *The Time Machine.* His hero moves forward through time, reaching a place that seems like paradise, in around the year 800,000. He finds that the apparently blissful humanoid Eloi, who are served by the fearsome Morlocks, are in fact being eaten by them. This was also an observation on a class system which separated the rich from the poor.

Since then, the genre has exploded, with a galactic multitude of magazines, comics, TV series, and movies thrown into the mix. Sci-fi can be exceptionally entertaining: Aliens! Robots! Invasions! Lasers! What's not to like?! It can also be exceptionally silly: *The Hitchhiker's Guide to the Galaxy* by Douglas Adams is one of the funniest books around, featuring a sad android called Marvin. Sci-fi can also be deeply serious. For example, Isaac Asimov's book *I, Robot,* was the first to explore how artificial intelligence might affect humanity and laid down the Three Laws of Robotics (see page 75).

## DISTORTING REALITY

In reflecting and distorting (i.e. twisting) our own world, sci-fi can help us understand it. One writer, Ursula K. Le Guin, wrote about a planet where humanoids could choose whether they became male or female for short periods of time. Utopian sci-fi lets us imagine how we might want the world to be. Dystopian sci-fi examines things we don't like. Rivers Solomon's *An Unkindness of Ghosts* sees a girl born into slavery on a spaceship, while *Who Fears Death* by Nnedi Okorafor is set in a

A TIME-TRAVELING DEVICE, SIMILAR TO THE ONE IN *THE TIME MACHINE* BY H.G. WELLS.

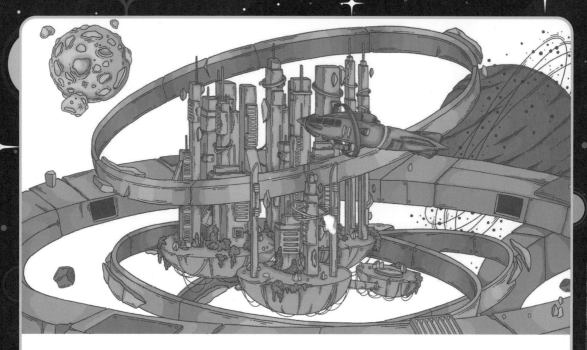

post-apocalyptic Africa. You might also have heard of Aldous Huxley's novel *Brave New World*, in which people are forbidden to have babies: instead they are "grown" in bottles.

Will tomorrow be better? Or worse? Maybe we humans can learn to control our own destiny, and progress will take us to wonderful places we can only dream of. Or maybe we'll be at the mercy of events and disasters we can't even yet imagine. The threat of nanobots, artificially engineered diseases, and nuclear war can sometimes feel overwhelming. Sci-fi warns us of the limits of progress as much as it wonders at it. Let's just hope that the Earth isn't destroyed to make way for a space highway, as in *The Hitchhiker's Guide to the Galaxy*. (And I don't much want to be invaded by giant space spiders, thank you very much.)

Sci-fi comes in as many shapes and sizes as there are planets in the galaxy. (Well, maybe not quite so many. That would be insane.) It is very much a genre that provides enormous amounts of scope for writers. And it works exceptionally well on the screen as well as on the page. You've probably seen at least one *Star Wars* movie. Frank Herbert's novel *Dune*, in which a young man, Paul Atreides, is sent with his family to a desert planet to mine a substance known as Spice, remains one of the most enchanting and engrossing sci-fi novels of all time. It's been made into two movies (one in 1984 by David Lynch, and one released in 2021, with Timothée Chalamet as Paul). Both movies are full of moments of wonder and awe. And giant sandworms.

## THE SCIENCE BEHIND SCI-FI

So, what makes sci-fi different from fantasy fiction? The important part is the science. Usually, sci-fi looks at scientific developments, and thinks about how they will change the way we live. You could think about geology—the study of rocks. Imagine finding a whole new

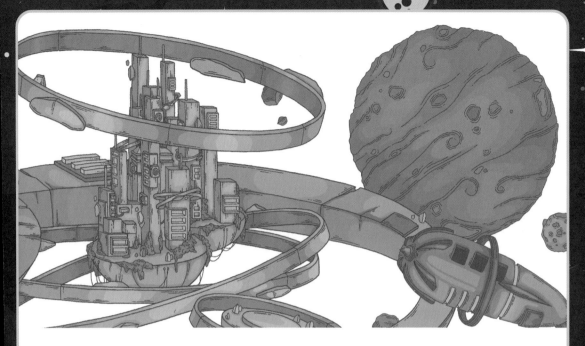

substance! Or archeology—you could dig up a weird dinosaur. Fantasy uses magic and monsters instead, without having much of a reason for it. Sci-fi tries to explain the magic. Or at least makes a stab at it, like the light sabers in *Star Wars*. Wave a wand and say a magic spell, and you've got fantasy. Wave a wand that alters the atoms of your enemy, and you've got sci-fi.

## READY TO WRITE SCI-FI?

Writing sci-fi uses all the same tools as writing any other genre. Just with fancier, shinier bits. And lasers. (Did I mention lasers?) You'll need to understand how to create solid characters—yes, even those daring heroes and deadly villains need to be believable—tightly controlled plots (no ending with "it was all a dream"), and brilliant, engrossing settings, from the wasted plains of Mars, through the burning mountains of Alpha Centauri and the red rivers of Magna Prime, to the edges of the known universe and

beyond. We'll discuss all of this, and more, in the pages that follow.

And you'll also need to be aware of all the many sub-genres and where you might want to fit into them. You'll get a sense of these, from the clockwork, steam-engine worlds of steampunk, through cyberpunk, utopias, dystopias, and all the way to the end of the world. You'll have a chance to think about your own world, and the things that make you tick. And the things that scare you, as well as the things that thrill and amaze you. The possibilities with sci-fi are, quite literally, out of this world.

So, strap on your jetpack and set your phasers to writing mode.

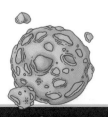

# WORLDBUILDING

CLOSE YOUR EYES. WAIT, HANG ON. NOW OPEN THEM AGAIN. OTHERWISE, YOU WON'T BE ABLE TO READ THIS. THERE YOU ARE. RIGHT, READ THIS SENTENCE NEXT: THINK OF ALL THE SCI-FI YOU HAVE READ IN COMICS OR BOOKS, OR SEEN ON TV OR AT THE MOVIES. NOW, THINK OF YOUR FAVORITE. CLOSE YOUR EYES AND KEEP THEM CLOSED FOR A GOOD TEN SECONDS OR SO.

**YOUR TEN SECONDS ARE UP.** What's the first thing that came into your mind? For most people it will be the new, strange, exotic, other worlds. I remembered Frank Herbert's *Dune* long after I read it (as a twelve-year-old), largely because of its worldbuilding: it describes a vast Empire, stretching across the known universe and controlling countless planets—including, of course, the desert planet itself, Arrakis.

Setting doesn't matter quite so much in normal fiction. If you write about a school in Los Angeles, it's not going to be hugely different from one in London. Sci-fi, on the other hand, is very much driven by where it's set. For many readers this is a way of escaping daily life. When you're staring out of the window at school, or on the bus, you can teleport yourself to other worlds entirely. . . .

## NUTS AND BOLTS

It's as important to get your world right as it is to make sure your spaceship's nuts and bolts have all been tightened before you blast off to Venus on a mining expedition.

You may have a Big Idea: a planet made up entirely of volcanoes, for example. Fine. Some people like to start big, with the world and the setting, and then work downward.

Others start with a smaller idea. For example, what would happen if you transplanted a school to a planet ravaged by six-headed mutant dinosaurs? And then work from there, building the world around it.

Either way, everything must fit together, and everything should make sense. You need to lay down the law. And you need to make sure that you stick to the laws. Don't mess with things or fudge them. Your readers will notice.

## THE SAME, BUT DIFFERENT

One thing you may be thinking is: well, hasn't everything been done before? And you may well be right. But that's nothing to worry about. We tend to like the same things. The floating island, Laputa, in Jonathan Swift's *Gulliver's Travels* has many descendants—the floating islands in the 2009 movie *Avatar*, for example. Some things never lose their power.

One of Philip Reeve's books for younger children, *Jinks & O'Hare, Funfair Repair*, is about an alien planet that's completely covered by a funfair. It's a lovely, funny story, in which a young girl stands up to a larger authority to save the planet. A few days after reading it, I found an old comic annual from my childhood. In it, there was a story about an alien planet which was entirely covered by a children's playground and where a young boy stood up to a larger authority to save it from destruction. Yes, there are only certain things that you can do with sci-fi: but it's *what* you do with them that counts. (And this goes for other forms of fiction too.)

## CREATOR OF WORLDS

So, what should you do when building your world? A good place to start is by looking at our own planet Earth. There are so many civilizations, species, microbes, and robots, plus a whole bunch of other things we probably don't even know about yet (did you know that nobody knows the details of how giant squid mate?). We already have things that appear completely outlandish, from vampire bats to fish with lights. We've got people living in all kinds of conditions, from ice cold to desert hot. We've had pretty much every system of government possible, at various times in history. And, of course, for most of our planet's lifetime, humans didn't even exist (the planet is about 4.5 billion years old and humans didn't appear until around 2 million years ago). It doesn't take long to isolate one of these elements and transplant it to a different world.

It's difficult to write about an entire planet with all its many differences. Some writers manage it. A lot of adult sci-fi goes in for very complicated worldbuilding, with entire planets imagined in all their tiniest details. But when you're starting out, it is worth using a smaller scale and sticking to one idea which you can develop further.

The more carefully and thoroughly you consider your other world, the better and more believable it will be. Some writers like to keep a whole worldbuilding document alongside their writing to refer back to, almost like their own encyclopedia.

It's entirely up to you how much of this you do. Some writers prefer to work out every last detail of their worlds, like Melinda Salisbury in *The Sin Eater's Daughter*. Others work as they write, preferring to leave some things unknown. Both methods have their advantages and disadvantages. An overworked world can feel flat on the page; conversely, a world that hasn't been fully considered can have gaps.

## TERRAFORMING

First things first: establish where your world is and consider how long your civilization has been there. Then, ask yourself the following questions (asking them will help you work out what kind of story you want to tell, and why):

- Do the people on your planet live in cities? Or on farms?
- Do they live above ground, below ground, in the oceans, or on space stations?
- How long have they been using technology?
- Does the planet communicate with other worlds?
- Who is in charge?
- What do they eat?
- What's the weather like?
- Do they keep pets?
- What do the schools look like?

Your world has to be believable. And the way to do this, my delightful intergalactic friends, is to make sure you think about the little things. It's how they cook their waffles in the morning. It's whether they go to school on a bus or a shuttle. The worst thing about bad sci-fi is when you get lots and lots of explanations just shoved in. One mistake writers make is to have characters tell each other what they already know. Don't do this. I'm telling you

now. It'll save you a lot of trouble. If you want your reader to know that there are two suns, don't write: "There were two suns on the planet Xplotts." Write: "As the first sun rose, Timo almost woke. It wasn't until the second sun's brighter beams were across his face that he fully awoke."

## CHARACTER IN SETTING

Once you've considered the makeup of your new world—its geography (draw a map if that helps), where your characters live, and so on—then you need to bring out the physical aspects they experience. One thing to bear in mind with sci-fi is that your characters may already be fully embedded in their world. Alternatively, you may be seeing this new world through the eyes of a stranger. Either approach will bring its own challenges, which we will look at in the *Character* chapter next.

Think about what you do every day. You don't wake up and say to yourself: "Oh, hey, there's my phone by my bedside with which

I tell the time and call friends and send messages and play games, and oh, I'm late for school."

No. Instead, you pick up your phone and scroll through it without thinking about it at all. Your characters also need to interact with the world around them in an unforced manner.

Let's think about a planet that's entirely underwater, as an example. Your humanoid inhabitants will have developed in a different way and have different routines and desires to us land-dwellers. Take a look at these examples:

### BAD EXAMPLE

"Snitha woke up in her bed. She stretched and yawned and picked up her breathing tube and her flippers which she had to wear to get to school on the aquabus. She switched on her radio and heard there was going to be a seastorm, which was annoying as that might make her late."

### BETTER EXAMPLE

"The sea was dark above Snitha when she woke. She switched on the bedside light. There was a slight smell of burning yogfish from below. Her mother must have forgotten to take her breakfast out of the oven.

She was almost asleep again when she remembered. Her deepdiving test. It was today. Two minutes later, she couldn't fit her breathing tube on. She wiggled it and wiggled it, and then threw it aside in frustration.

Through the thick glass window, she could see that all the betafish had vanished, and the mareweed was moving to mysterious currents.

That was always a bad sign.

The intercom buzzed.

*'Hurry up, Snitha!'*

It was her mother. The aquabus must be waiting. Scrambling, she managed to click on the tube, and was into her flippers before it buzzed again."

## IT'S ALL IN THE DETAIL

Remember, all the way through, we need to be hitting those recognizable senses. Your protagonist (see page 41) should reflect human needs and desires, even if they are not technically human. Your protagonist will eat things for breakfast, whether they're pills or bear-meat or computer code. Your transport systems may be old and creaky and charming, or they may be new and shiny, but they will have their own smells and damaged seats and passengers with their own quirks.

Focus, with laser-like attention, on details. It will be these that your readers remember. In Frank Herbert's *Dune*, for example, the opening section shows us Castle Caladan, the home of Paul Atreides. There's not much to suggest that we're in a future world—until we're shown a floating lamp. This is the wow moment we're looking for.

Now go ahead and find your own wow moment—the universe is your luminous, spice-eating, mega-sized oyster.

# WORLDBUILDING PLAN

PLANET NAME:
................................................................................
................................................................................

SYSTEM NAME:
................................................................................

GALAXY:
................................................................................

INTELLIGENT INHABITANTS:
................................................................................
................................................................................
................................................................................

PLANTS:
................................................................................
................................................................................
................................................................................

ANIMALS:
................................................................................
................................................................................
................................................................................

CITIES:

.............................................................................................................................................

.............................................................................................................................................

.............................................................................................................................................

.............................................................................................................................................

MAJOR POLITICAL SYSTEMS:

.............................................................................................................................................

.............................................................................................................................................

.............................................................................................................................................

SCHOOLING SYSTEM:

.............................................................................................................................................

.............................................................................................................................................

.............................................................................................................................................

GEOGRAPHY:

.............................................................................................................................................

.............................................................................................................................................

.............................................................................................................................................

AGE OF CIVILIZATION:

.............................................................................................................................................

.............................................................................................................................................

.............................................................................................................................................

LEVEL OF TECHNOLOGY:

.............................................................................................................................................

.............................................................................................................................................

.............................................................................................................................................

FOODSTUFFS:

.............................................................................................................................................

.............................................................................................................................................

.............................................................................................................................................

# OUT OF THIS WORLD

**PLANET EARTH,** vast and bustling though it is on the surface, can feel infinitely alone. Astronauts often speak of this feeling: of the preciousness of our habitat, floating in space, so blue, so rare. When, in Milton's long epic poem *Paradise Lost*, Satan flies through space to Earth (the first astronaut?), he sees our "frail world" and believes it to be "hanging in a golden chain."

## EACH PLANET HAS ITS OWN STORY

We are both splendidly isolated, and yet part of something amazingly vast. Since Copernicus and Galileo proved to us that we revolve around the Sun, our sense of our place in the universe has shifted. We have not been the center of the universe for centuries. Maybe we are even on the edge of it. As writer Douglas Adams said: Earth is "a small, blue-green world in one of the less fashionable sectors of the galaxy." But we want to know what's out there. Our solar system is a richly varied place with

many locations to set a sci-fi story. There are eight (no, seven, since poor old Pluto was demoted) other planets to play with, not to mention their assorted moons, hangers-on, and asteroids. Every single object that can be landed on in the solar system is a potential source of a narrative. You could even set a story on the Asteroid Belt.

Think about how many planets there are in the Milky Way. Not enough for you? Then perhaps in the neighboring galaxy, Andromeda. Still too tame? Then widen your scope into the whole universe. There are probably around 50 galaxies in our local group. There are around 100,000 galaxies in our Local Supercluster. And as for the whole universe. . . . The answer to the question is so staggeringly enormous that it makes everyone's head spin. Even the scientists. There is every possible galaxy, perhaps with thousands of habitable planets, or planets that could host some kind of life, or that could be transformed into planets for humans to live on.

Let's start closer to home. *Mars Evacuees* by Sophia McDougall is about a group of children sent to Mars to escape an alien attack. Here, they're meant to be trained up for war. But nothing goes to plan. Kevin Emerson's *Last Day on Mars* sees the colonized planet about to be swallowed up by the Sun. So, hero Liam has to set off to find a more habitable planet.

Pretty much every planet in the solar system has been explored in this way. You could set a city on Mercury (hot!). Philip Reeve's *Larklight* sees humans on the moons of Jupiter. It's the same in *The Jupiter Pirates: Hunt for the Hydra* by Jason Fry, where kid pirates go off on an amazing adventure. You could even send your brave characters all the way out to old, cold Pluto himself (yes, I still count him as a planet) where you might find intelligent beings even in the most terrifying settings. And that's just on our doorstep. If planets can have doorsteps. Well, you know what I mean.

One of the best things about keeping your sci-fi story close to Earth is that you can compare and contrast it with the other planets. The fertility and diversity of our planet seems remarkably inviting when you're crawling across the frozen plains of Pluto, the Sun far distant, and no such thing as leaves. You can invest your characters with memories of their home lives in cities, forests, or by the sea.

## CREATING YOUR OTHER WORLD

**1.** Decide what you want to focus on. Do you want loads of tech? Or do you want to write about people?

**2.** Choose your time period. Are you in the near future? Could it be the first colonizers of the Moon or Mars? Are we dealing with a catastrophe on Earth that has sent people looking for the nearest planet? Or are we in the far future, where Earth is the ancient center of a huge interstellar network, and the solar system has been fully colonized?

**3A.** Do you want to have your characters explore this new world? There's a lot to think about here. You've got all the dangers and delights of a new world. Think about what your characters want. Do they want a new home? Somewhere safe, away from danger? Or do they want to find treasure? Or even bring an end to a war? Think about what might be on the planet that could help them do this. Is there a precious metal on the moons of Jupiter? And who else is after it?

**3B.** Now. Think about who's already on the planet. How will your explorers interact with them? Will they be friendly, or hostile? There's plenty of room for great storytelling here, as your characters deal with the indigenous peoples, and vice versa.

**4A.** If you want to go farther afield, you have several options. One is to have humans invading, exploring, or colonizing a new planet.

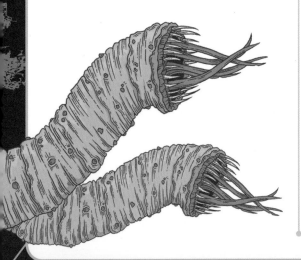

This was very much the old *Star Trek* trope (see page 23): the starship *Enterprise* boldly goes and finds a new planet, then beams some people down. They get into trouble, solve a problem, return to the ship, and there you have it, everyone can go home and have a nice dinner.

**4B.** You can play with this idea. You could tell your story from the point of view of the colonized planet. Similarly, Frank Herbert's *Dune* sees many fully formed planets inhabited by humans and human-like creatures, with nary a mention of Earth. You could have a planet which was colonized long ago by Earth humans. So long ago that they've forgotten everything about their old ways and technologies. They might start acting more like medieval people.

**5.** Another approach to worldbuilding is to create a planet that is completely untouched by humans. This offers enormous possibilities for building your own world from (literally) the ground up. You can invent any kind of society you like. Underground cave-people, sophisticated palace dwellers, sea-people, centaurs. Aliens with three eyes and four noses. Things that are made of color and gas. Just remember, you still need to tell a story. A character who wants something, and a character who's stopping that from happening. A plot that begins and finishes. Go wild—but within reason.

So what are you waiting for? Get your telescope out and search the stars.

# PLANETS: WRITING PROMPTS

**1. GREED IS GOOD, RIGHT?** A gold mine is discovered on the Moon, offering untold riches. Across the globe, a race begins to get there first. A young scientist is offered a position on one of the first rockets going to the Moon, but discovers that there are nefarious things going on. . . .

**2. SOLAR EMPIRE** The solar system has been ruled for centuries by a dying empire, based on the planets Earth and terraformed (see page 22) Mars. But one lonely asteroid is home to a rapidly growing rebellion. . . .

**3. IT'S ALL PHYSICAL** Imagine an instruction manual for launching a successful invasion: try writing the general's strategy.

**4. HOW THE MIGHTY FALL** Write down the first eight words that occur to you after you hear the word "FIRE." Now describe a landscape using those eight words.

**5. HOME AWAY FROM HOME** You wake up one morning to find a door in your house that wasn't there before. When you go through it, you come out into a different world and find that your house has been transformed into an enormous version of itself. Describe your feelings.

**6. ODE FROM PLUTO** Imagine you're a poet living on Pluto. Write about the Sun from your new perspective—remember how far away you are!

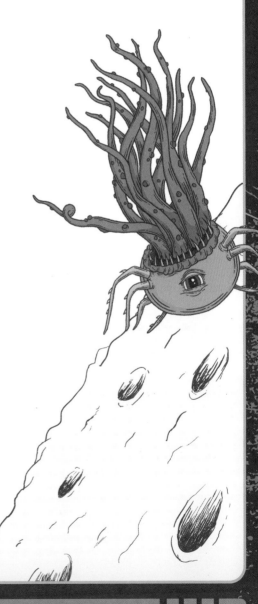

## KEY WORD

TERRAFORMING
Where another planet
is altered in order to
make it Earth-like.

**KEY WORD**
TROPE
A significant or recurrent theme. A recognizable plot device used to tell a story. Like the cape being the main element of a superhero costume.

**WATER ON MARS**
Scientists believe that Mars
was once covered in water.
Did the planet support life?

**FAR OUT**

*Oumuamua* is a mysterious interstellar object observed at the farthest reaches of the solar system.

# UTOPIAS

**THE WORD UTOPIA** is usually taken to mean "a good place," and originates from the Greek *eu-topia*. But Sir Thomas More—the 15th-century writer who made up the word—was, in fact, making a joke because it actually comes from the Greek *ou-topia*, which means "no such place." (Yes, I can see you laughing. Come on, it's funny! No? OK, never mind.)

Sir Thomas More's *Utopia* describes a society on an island where all goods are held in common. There are no locks on the doors and people change their houses every ten years. Sounds like a barrel of laughs, right?

OK, this might not be everybody's idea of fun, but then More wasn't necessarily describing a society he thought was possible. That hasn't stopped the word utopia being used to describe ideal societies which are, or should be, fully possible, or which their writers wish were possible.

Those utopias tend to fall into two types: ones in which everything is joyful and festive and those in which everything's a bit, well, sensible and boring. (You should think very carefully about which one you want. And it shouldn't be the latter.)

## TROUBLE IN PARADISE

And there, in terms of narrative, is the difficulty with utopias. If everything is fine and happy and nothing ever goes wrong, then there's no possibility of conflict or danger, and so no possibility of good fiction. This idea powers *The Giver* by Lois Lowry, in which a young boy in a utopian society free from all ills is bestowed with the memories of history. As a result, he grows increasingly unhappy with his dull society.

So, think very carefully about the rules of your utopian society. Try asking yourself the following questions:

- How was the utopia built?
- Who constructed it and why?
- What was it created to stop?
- Can we believe that humans would be so fully invested in this society to keep it going?
- What is keeping the utopia from falling apart right now?

Have you ever seen the 2015 movie *Tomorrowland*? In this, a futuristic utopia is dedicated to the development of science. The world's greatest thinkers and dreamers are recruited from Earth to work there. When a powerful machine predicts the end of the world and the mayor of Tomorrowland closes his doors, the utopia is under threat. (I won't give any spoilers away, don't worry.) Another good way of dealing with the problem is to have your utopia facing a threat from other people or beings who don't care about the carefully tended ideals of your civilization.

Most utopias in fiction, then, are not actually utopias at all. We are back to the idea of a "no-place." They often have sinister or troubling aspects. Where they differ from dystopias (see the next section) is that in general the society is at least trying to move toward a better place. There are plenty of opportunities for this. Let's have a look at some of them.

## CREATING YOUR UTOPIA

**1.** Think about how people live today and consider these examples:

- We have our own possessions. What about a world in which nobody owned anything?
- We're always thinking about the future. You're probably thinking about your test next week, or your hockey game, or your trip to see your grandmother. But what if we never thought about the future? Imagine a world where people just lived in the moment.
- Think about what your life would be like if everything was done by robots.
- You could think about putting Earth cultures onto a different planet. Imagine a traditional African culture, for example, on a terraformed planet, or one that only cowboys migrated to. (Perhaps, to make room for more people, all of Earth's cattle have been transported to another planet fertile with grass.)

BUILD A WORLD AS CRAZY AND IMAGINATIVE AS YOU LIKE! YOU COULD HAVE LOLLIPOP BUILDINGS AND FLOATING CRYSTALS IN THE SKY.

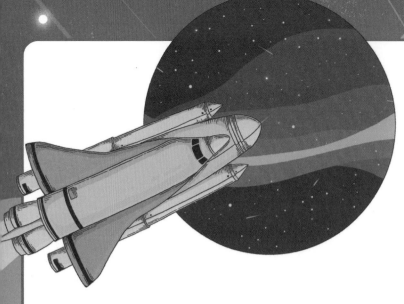

GET IN YOUR
SPACESHIP AND FLY
AWAY TO A UTOPIA OF
YOUR DREAMS. . . .

**2.** You can also draw on your own experiences. In E. Nesbit's classic novel *The Story of the Amulet*, the Edwardian protagonists travel far into the future, finding a London which is entirely free from smoke and where manual workers are as well rewarded and housed as the rich. The children meet a boy who's been expelled from school for the day. Rather than enjoying himself, he's absolutely devastated because he loves school. This would have been strange to Nesbit's readers (and may even, despite many years of progressive schooling policies, be strange to you). Nesbit's school readers would have endured harsh discipline.

**3.** As always, look around carefully at your surroundings. You may live in the city, in the countryside, in the suburbs. You could be living in a farmhouse on the edge of a plain, or at the top of a skyscraper in the busiest city in the world. If you look, you'll see where you can identify injustice, or unfairness, or simply something that could be changed to make things better. You can also research attempts to build utopian communities here on Earth.

**4.** You can also project further than your own immediate surroundings. Think about and look at these bigger issues:

- The effects of technology—do advances in technology automatically create a utopia? What if no one could die because of a machine? See Prompt 5 on page 30 to explore this idea further.

- What sacrifices must humans make to create a better world? Climate change is one of the burning issues of our time, but what must humanity do to avoid it? A utopian world in which nobody uses fossil fuels would bring up all sorts of interesting conundrums. Peter Dickinson's series, The Changes, sees a United Kingdom which is entirely thrown back into a utopian medieval past where no technology will work. The trilogy ends with the sound of a gasoline engine starting. Is this a good thing, or bad?

Utopian novels ask interesting questions. Keep asking them—and you will discover some fascinating answers.

# UTOPIAS: WRITING PROMPTS

**1. COMING OF AGE** What does it mean to become an adult in your utopian society? Write down three coming-of-age ceremonies you've heard of (bar mitzvah, confirmation, and graduation, for example). Think about the actions and symbols of each, and what ideals and values they promote. Now construct a coming-of-age ceremony around the ideals and values you want to show in your utopia.

**2. FEEL THE FEAR** Once you've come up with your ceremony from Prompt 1, write a scene in which your protagonist is scared to go ahead with the ceremony, but eventually decides to go through with it.

**3. LOSING CONFIDENCE** Now flip Prompt 2, so that your protagonist is initially confident, but then becomes more frightened. What avenues for your story does this approach open up? It's all relative.

**4. FAMILY VALUES** How does family life work in your utopia? Are the kids adopted? Do extended families live together? Write about an extended family in the year 3024. You're on the planetary space station Excelsior, in orbit around the gas giant Marine 5. Write a diary log about the day a school inspector comes to check on your school.

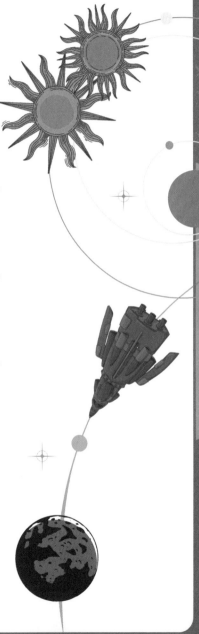

**5. THE ILLS OF SOCIETY** No world is problem-free. Imagine one in which any of the following have been removed: poverty, illness, or death, or pick your own. What would the consequences be? Build a character that has never heard of death. Now put them on a hunting expedition out into the stars, where one of the hunters is fatally wounded. Or a character that has never heard of illness. Send them to a hospital on another planet. Then write a letter home in the voice of the protagonist, describing this moment.

**6. EDUCATION, EDUCATION, EDUCATION** You love school, right? No? You don't? Well then, imagine your perfect school. Does it have loads of tech? Can you choose your own classes? Is there no discipline? Write down a list of ten things you'd like to see. Now, write a scene from the perspective of a teacher giving a lesson in your perfect classroom. What's that you say? There are no teachers in your perfect school? In that case, describe one of the students breaking a rule. What are the consequences of this?

**7. THE IDEAL WORLD** Write down your three favorite activities: eating ice cream, going to the zoo, playing computer games. Whatever you like. Construct a city in which you can do all these things, however many times you like. What problems would arise? Write a scene in the first person in which having enough of what you like becomes too much.

**8. DISRUPTION** Pick one of the following: a paradise moon orbiting the planet Jupiter, a luxury spaceship inhabited by wealthy aliens, or an expensive hotel with views over a nebula. Now write a scene in which a fancy dinner is disrupted by some terrible news.

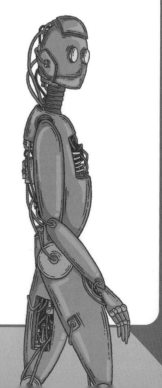

**KEY WORD**

ANARCHY
Often taken
to mean chaos,
but it, in fact,
simply means
"without rule."

**KEY WORDS**

CRYOGENIC SUSPENSION
This is when the body is
preserved though low-
temperature freezing.

# DYSTOPIAS

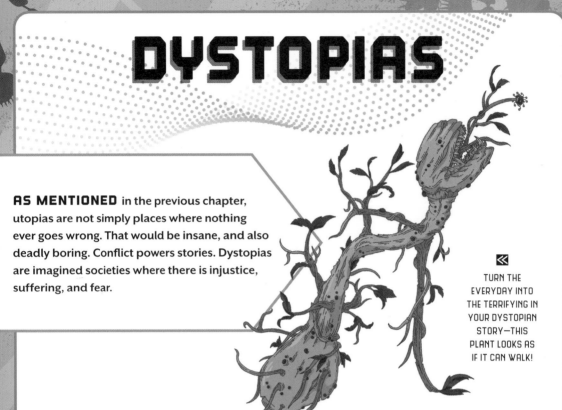

**AS MENTIONED** in the previous chapter, utopias are not simply places where nothing ever goes wrong. That would be insane, and also deadly boring. Conflict powers stories. Dystopias are imagined societies where there is injustice, suffering, and fear.

TURN THE EVERYDAY INTO THE TERRIFYING IN YOUR DYSTOPIAN STORY—THIS PLANT LOOKS AS IF IT CAN WALK!

Now, it may seem strange to mention the children's author Beatrix Potter here, in a book about writing sci-fi, but hear me out. Readers often remember her book *The Tale of Peter Rabbit* (and the rest of her books) as lovely, safe spaces where sweet little animals live adorable, cuddly lives in blissful freedom, like Sylvanian Families. In fact, the worlds of Beatrix Potter are far from utopian. They are full of threats, naughtiness, and menace. Peter Rabbit's father was eaten by Mr. McGregor. Squirrel Nutkin gets his tail bitten off by the owl, and it doesn't change him a bit. That's what makes the stories so memorable.

Recent years have seen an explosion in dystopian fiction. *Dystopia* simply means "bad place," the opposite of *eu-topia* (good place), not *ou-topia* (no-place). Dystopias look at the troubles in our world, and instead of imagining how to get rid of them, push them as far as they can go. Like utopias, they can tell us what the author's beliefs are.

As a result, dystopias can be deeply and effectively terrifying, particularly if they describe things close to home. Usually, dystopias will deal with disasters or problems we can already imagine: how people's identities are affected by technology, for example, or how governments can become excessive in their attempts to control the population. Even climate change has spawned its own sub-sub-genre (which is known as cli-fi).

# TYPES OF DYSTOPIAS

Let's look at some different types of dystopias, centered around everything, from technology to politics to comedy.

**1.** People have been thinking about technology forever. Here are a few fictional examples:

- Tony DiTerlizzi's *The Search for Wondla* tells a story of a young girl living underground, and being raised by a robot. She has not seen another human her whole life, and only knows of the outside world through holograms.
- Aldous Huxley's *Brave New World*, perhaps the most famous dystopia of all, in which families are banned, everyone spends their leisure time doing government-approved activities, and babies are born in bottles in factories. Terrifying!
- Sally Gardner's *Maggot Moon* sees a future in which Britain is run by an oppressive government. Young Standish Treadwell is contacted by a band of rebels who have to make a stand.
- Catherine Fisher's *Incarceron* is set in a complicated, high-tech prison. Finn is kept locked up there, and somehow manages to connect to the outside world through a crystal key.
- Cloned dinosaurs take over the planet in Laura Martin's *Edge of Extinction: The Ark Plan,* so humans have to move underground. When Sky finds out about her missing father, she has to go up to the surface—and finds out the truth.
- *The Line* by Teri Hall—the United States is at war. Rachel is a young girl who lives near The Line, which is the boundary between them and Away. One day, she connects with someone from the other side, and uncovers what's really going on.

THE ROMANCE OF
THE WORLD IN RUINS
—OVERGROWN AND
CRUMBLING, BUT STILL
STRANGELY BEAUTIFUL.

**2.** Dystopias can also be deeply political, as in George Orwell's novel *Nineteen Eighty-Four*, which warns us of the perils of communism (this is when individual people cannot own things like land; instead, the government or the whole community owns them).

**3.** Dystopias don't have to be serious: one of my favorite children's authors, Diana Wynne Jones, wrote a wonderfully funny novel called *The Dark Lord of Derkholm*, in which an entire planet is held captive by a demon and used as an adventure camp for tourists. It makes you think about the destruction that tourism can bring.

**4.** You can project as far into the future as you like.

- How about a world in which technology has managed to make your dreams literally change the world? What if you were forced to dream of war—or peace? Or giant flying goldfish? Ronald Kidd's *Dreambender* is about a group of "dreambenders" who enter people's dreams at night, and take away any thoughts they think are a problem. What if people woke up one day with their memories removed?
- What about a world in which machines have taken over? In *The Last Human* by Lee Bacon, robots have gotten rid of humans entirely. Or have they?
- What about a future in which teenagers are sent to fight to the death in front of a baying audience? Where reality TV shows are taken too far, as observed in The Hunger Games by Suzanne Collins, a series of books and movies that you've probably read or seen.

THE MOCKINGJAY FROM SUZANNE COLLINS' THE HUNGER GAMES SERIES.

Each of these dystopian books or movies is commenting on some aspect of the world: *The Hunger Games* looks at why we enjoy other people's troubles, and what happens when some people get too much power. *Dreambender* plays with our ideas of what reality is. *The Last Human* makes us think about what it means to be flesh and blood and alive.

The risk with dystopian fiction is precisely the opposite of that with utopian fiction. It can be too grim, too gloomy, too downbeat. You don't want to make things seem too inescapable, too pointless. For this reason, we need to include lively, interesting characters, rich details, and a fast-moving plot that allow us to hope for resolution and change.

Are you ready to get down and dirty? Then let's delve into dystopias . . . and if you want to try a dystopian version of *The Tale of Peter Rabbit*—well, I for one would be delighted to see the results.

# DYSTOPIAS: WRITING PROMPTS

**1. ANTISOCIAL MEDIA** Social media is how you contact your friends and how you find out about movies and books. It's on your phone in your pocket, on your laptop, and on your tablet. And it knows everything about you. It's fine, right now. But what if it all goes wrong?

In a not-too-distant future, social media is being used by governments to keep tabs on its citizens. Your fingerprint and photographs are taken from your social media networks and used to create a clone account. This account starts committing some serious crimes in your name. . . . You're having dinner one night when the doorbell rings. It's the police. Write what happens next. . . .

**2. SIX THINGS I HATE ABOUT TECH**
Technology has been advancing at a rapid pace. Sometimes, this can be frightening. Write down the first six things that come into your head. Now go further and describe a futuristic city where this technology has taken over.

**3. FAMILY FORTUNES** In a near-dystopian future, children are separated from their parents at birth. Use your own hometown as the setting. Against the rules of society, you seek out your mother and father. Write a scene where you see someone on the street who you think might be your father. Focus on the sights, sounds, and smells. Don't use any dialogue.

**4. CLI-FI** Sea levels are rising. Your house is on top of a hill. Describe a day when the sea flows inland, turning your hill into an island. You and your family are safe. But your enemy is in a boat, approaching with his mother, father, and younger sister. What do you do?

**5. RISE OF THE CLONES** You come home from school one day to find that not only have your parents cloned you, but your clone has also moved in and will be staying with you for a while. Write a diary entry of the family dinner that night.

**6. THE OPPRESSOR OPPRESSED** You are living in an oppressed city. Your mother is one of the president's closest advisers. One night you find a secret that could bring the president down and free the people of the city.

**7. ROMEO AND JULIET** You are a member of a powerful family in a dystopian future. You fall in love with one of the children of the opposition families. Describe the moment when you meet outside, against the rules. Avoid any dialogue and focus on the senses.

**WATCH OUT, WORLD**
Many technological advances imagined in dystopian fiction have come true, from machine facial recognition to manufactured meat.

# TRANSPORTATION

**IN A SENSE,** planet Earth is a spaceship, traveling through space, and we are all astronauts. We'd love, however, to see what's out there. Only, how do we get there? You can't just hail a space-taxi. (Yet. Although I bet there are plans for that one.)

Currently, our own manned spaceships can't really reach much farther than the Moon. As for space probes—well, they take ages to get anywhere. The probe *Voyager I* was launched in 1977 and only reached interstellar space (see page 49) in 2021.

Spaceships are therefore crucial to writing good sci-fi: the *Millennium Falcon* (*Star Wars*), and the starship *Enterprise* (*Star Trek*) both evoke awe and wonder. The sense that they are forging through the universe over vast distances into the unknown is extraordinary. There are, of course, different kinds of transportation vessels to explore and use. Jules Verne's novel *From the Earth to the Moon* uses a space capsule launched by a gun. (Better hope it hits!)

So, how do you decide on the type of transportation system? Here are some ideas:

**1.** First things first: understand the type of transport you want. There are space stations that circle around planets, reached by shuttles. There are small rockets that go to moons. There are larger vessels that fly between planets. Then there are even bigger ones between stars or galaxies. There are military ships, hospital ships, colonizing ships, mining ships. . . . In Douglas Adams' *The Hitchhikers' Guide to the Galaxy*, for example, an entire ship is filled with what are thought to be useless people like insurance salesmen, meant to be sent to their doom, only for it to crash onto planet Earth.

**2.** Think about the huge distances. The fact that the universe is so large means you need to consider ways of getting around it that seem believable. From star drives to warp drives to nuclear fission, anything is possible. In Brandon Sanderson's Skyward series, there are people with the ability to jump from one point in space to another. Think about what could have made this possible in humans. Another way to get round the problems of unimaginable distances is to have the crew put into cryogenic suspension (see page 35), so they don't wake up until they get there. Plenty of room for trouble there. . . .

**3.** Your vessel could be its own world. This can provide many opportunities for fiction. You might set an entire book on a spaceship—like in Philip Reeve's *Cakes in Space*, in which a family boards a ship and goes into cryogenic suspended animation. The daughter of the family wakes up before she's meant to—and discovers that the ship has been taken over by giant killer cakes. You could even think about having a ship that's alive and that makes its own decisions.

**4.** And that's only the start of it. You can use pretty much any kind of transport you like. And who doesn't like trains? Ever since Alice got on a train in Lewis Carroll's *Through the Looking-Glass*, they've been a powerful force in fiction—E. Nesbit certainly knew this when she wrote her classic novel, *The Railway Children*. My favorite sci-fi series more recently has been Philip Reeve's *Railhead*, in which intergalactic sentient trains travel through special gates.

**5.** This brings us to the idea of wormholes. Also known as Einstein-Rosen bridges (because Albert Einstein's Relativity Theory predicts their existence), these are passages through space-time that allow travel from one end of the universe to the other. This is how people travel in the popular *Stargate* series. With wormholes, you need to devise rules for what can go in and out. A "stargate" is only open for a short amount of time, for example. And, perhaps most dazzling of all, there is the Closed Timelike Curve, in which a traveler is able to pass anywhere along their own timeline.

» SPIRAL THROUGH A WORMHOLE TO A DIFFERENT WORLD— HOPEFULLY, YOU'LL BE ABLE TO GET BACK AGAIN.

**b.** If the ocean is home to giant squid and whales, then there's no reason why space shouldn't be full of enormous floating animals that can be harnessed for transportation reasons. Terry Pratchett's Discworld novels famously take place on the back of a giant space turtle. In an episode of the TV series *Doctor Who*—"The Beast Below"—the population of planet Earth is evacuated onto a Star Whale, almost like the one below.

Whatever you do, stick to the rules of your world. Pink flying centaurs the size of Mars might work in some stories, but in others, you'll need the cold, hard, plausible detail of science. Now, three, two, one. . . . Liftoff!

# TRANSPORTATION: WRITING PROMPTS

**1. GO BOLDLY** Design a spaceship from the ground up. Who's building it? How big is it? Where is it going? What is its mission? Describe its moment of liftoff, from the perspective of the captain. Introduce something troubling just as the ship is leaving the atmosphere.

**2. GIANT SPACE BATS** Scribble down the first four animals that come into your head. Make one of them a giant space traveler. Saddle up for a journey to Alpha Centauri. Describe the moment your space beast becomes tired. What do you do?

**3. THE LONGEST JOURNEY** Imagine a spaceship preparing for a light year's long journey to a far-flung planet. Describe a young child's impressions, focusing on the sights, sounds, smells, and tastes.

**4. THRUST OF THE MATTER** Think of three plausible fuels for your spaceship. Now, imagine a scenario where you're on the ship, the fuel's running out, and there's no way to get any more. . . . Write down, in the first person, a scene where you are a passenger trying to find out what's going on.

**5. WORMHOLES** You live on a distant, newly inhabited planet that can only be reached by wormhole. One day, the wormhole gate closes for no reason. You are cut off from news, medicine, and provisions. Write a scene in which a character tells a more important person that the wormhole has closed down.

**6. PLANNING IT OUT** You're taking a cargo of allonium to a distant spaceport, with three refueling stops, and you must avoid the Ooolvian Belt pirates. Plan the journey, noting what you need and how you'll get it there.

**7. INTRUDER ALERT** You are on a vessel with three friends, returning home. Everything is fine. Until your computer system tells you there's someone else on board. . . .

**8. RACE THE MILKY WAY** A prize mining job lies in wait on the Asteroid Belt, but another company is going to reach it first. Describe how you get past the other ship.

## KEY WORDS

GENERATION SHIP
A spaceship that takes hundreds or even thousands of years to reach its final destination. The original astronauts will have died by the end of the journey.

INTERSTELLAR SPACE
The place where the
Sun's flow of energy
and magnetic field
stop affecting its
surroundings.

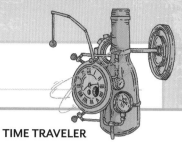

**TIME TRAVELER**
An English Heritage plaque on a house in London records the existence of Jacob von Hogflume (1864–1909), the inventor of time travel, living at the house in 2189. It's a joke, obviously. (Or is it?)

# CYBERPUNK AND STEAMPUNK

## A KEY DIFFERENCE
between these sub-genres is the time in which the stories take place. Cyberpunk tends to be set in the near future, often in a dystopian world, while steampunk is usually set in the past and looks at an alternative history.

Taking each sub-genre in turn, you will find that cyberpunk draws from human countercultures like punks and computer hackers. Some of the action may happen in the real world, while some of it takes place in "cyberspace" or within the world of computers. Its aesthetics have become normalized and are widely used within computer games, movies, and graphic novels. You may have seen the 2017 movie *Blade Runner 2049*—that's a great example of cyberpunk's combination of gritty societies and advanced technology. Think rain, dirty streets, people with terrible secrets, and malfunctioning machines. Not just a Friday night in your local town. The genre has developed into many forms, and is still hugely influential.

William Gibson's *Neuromancer* is one of the earliest and best examples of cyberpunk, and it tends to be written mostly for adults and young adults. Cory Doctorow's *Little Brother* is a great YA cyberpunk, about computer hackers, and *Warcross* by Marie Lu sees a hacker hunting down criminals. The major characteristic of this sub-genre is that humans are set against a society that doesn't much care for them. For this reason, you'll often find them in *Dystopias* (see pages 36–43).

Steampunk, on the other hand, tends to be set in the past—usually in the 19th century. It imagines an alternative history, in which technology took a different path. And quite often steam-powered inventions are used. Tim Powers was one of this sub-genre's earliest writers, using Victorian London as a backdrop to tales of time travel and black magic.

More recently, Philip Reeve has created a steampunk universe in his Larklight series. Larklight is the name of a house that orbits in space, and the young Victorian protagonists zip about the solar system. Even more recently, there is an entire Manga series called Clockwork Planet by Yuu Kamiya and Tsubaki Himana, and illustrated by Shino, which is set on an Earth where everything is run by clockwork.

Steampunk has a huge and devoted following: many people like to dress up as steampunk characters, and there are steampunk festivals across the world. It's so appealing because it mixes historical elements and scientific ones: what could be more fun than the thought of Sherlock Holmes with a clockwork automaton instead of Watson? Or Abraham Lincoln as an alien-hunting assassin?

# CYBERPUNK AND STEAMPUNK: WRITING PROMPTS

**1. SHERCLOCK HOLMES** Choose your favorite 19th-century characters. Now turn them into a series of clockwork automatons.

**2. E.T., TELEGRAPH HOME** Find a 19th- century historical event. The coronation of Queen Victoria? The assassination of Abraham Lincoln? Now, introduce some aliens.

**3. EMO 4 EVA** Think about some of the sub-cultures you know. Perhaps punk, goth, or emo. Describe what characterizes one of them. Imagine your sub-culture 20 years in the future.

**4. STEAM IT UP** Pick one of the following: cell phone, printer, airplane. Now, imagine if it ran on steam power.

**5. A-CLOCK-ALYPSE NOW** Mix things up a bit: imagine a future in which electricity is unavailable and we all have to rely on steam for power instead. Write a diary entry from the point of view of a kid.

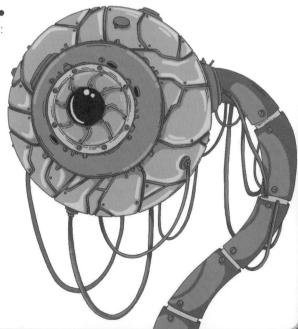

ORIGINS
Steampunk was coined
by K. W. Jeter in 1987.

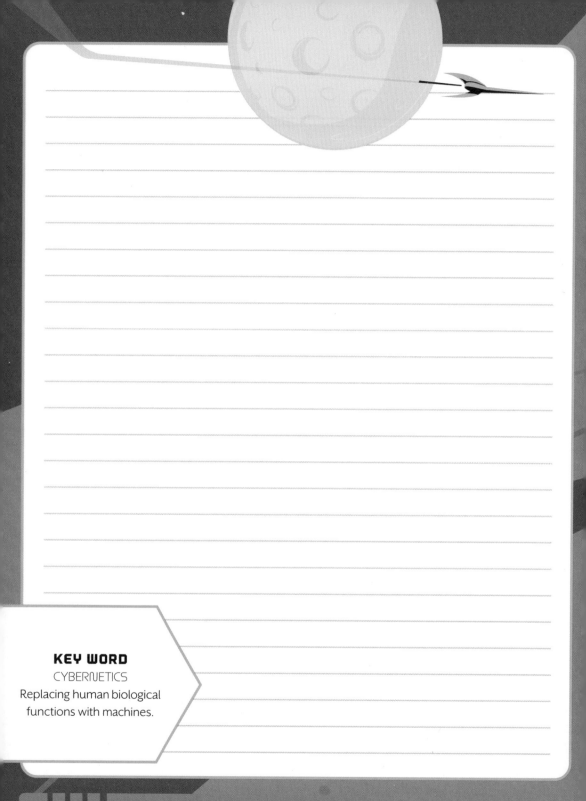

## KEY WORDS
STREAM OF CONSCIOUSNESS
A style of writing that tries to capture the natural flow of a character's thought process.

## WHO ARE YOU CALLING PUNK?

The writer Bruce Bethke came up with the word "cyberpunk" in a short story of the same name.

# CHARACTER

IT CAN BE EASY, WHEN WRITING SCI-FI, TO FORGET ABOUT CHARACTER: AFTER ALL, IT'S THE SETTING THAT COUNTS, ISN'T IT? THOSE GORGEOUS SUNSETS OVER THE SINGING MOUNTAINS OF VARONIA, AS THE WINGED ELDER-BEASTS PERFORM THEIR THROATY HARMONIES, AND THE MANY-COLORED, MULTI-EYED, RAVENOUS BEASTS OF THE BOOLIAN PLANETARY SYSTEM CHASE THEIR OWN TAILS! NOT TO MENTION THE EXPLOSIONS, THE NEBULAS, THE ASTEROID SHOWERS, AND THE SUPERNOVAS. . . .

**IT'S TRUE** that in a lot of sci-fi, characters fall into easily defined types, or even stereotypes. There is the bluff, daring protagonist (see page 41) and the archetypal (see page 71) evil villain, like Katniss Everdeen and President Snow, or Luke Skywalker and Darth Vader.

This doesn't mean that you should fall into the same patterns, however—unless you really want to and you're having fun with the idea. There's plenty of room for creating well-developed and intriguing characters. *Ikenga* by Nnedi Okorafor sees 11-year-old Nnamdi bringing to justice the man who murdered his father. Nnamdi gets the ability to shapeshift. Eden Royce's *Root Magic* sees young Jezebel learning the magic her family has done for generations. *Dragon Pearl* by Yoon Ha Lee mixes science fiction with Korean mythology, and has an adventurous young female protagonist.

Character is just as important in sci-fi as it is in any other genre, and as in any other genre, you should use the same techniques to develop your characters and help your readers get to know them. After all, even Darth Vader, the main antagonist in the original trilogy of *Star Wars*, has a backstory. (Just make sure to watch the films in release order and not chronological order.) So, how do you go about establishing your character?

## CRAFTING YOUR CHARACTER

**1.** First of all, as explained in the *Worldbuilding* chapter (see page 12), readers need to understand your protagonist within their setting. Some people like to draw up mini biographies for this. If your main character grew up on the distant moons of Jupiter, for example, you might ask the following questions:

- How does your character think about Earth?
- How has the world around your character helped shape them? What do they want? What do they need?
- What do their parents want? Is this different from what your character wants?
- What kinds of foods are available? Do they live on algae and rats? If so, why?

**2.** Creating your world will help you to create your character. Think about why your protagonist ended up on this world, and ask some more questions:

- Was your character born on this world or on another?
- Are they invaders or invaded? Powerful, or powerless?
- What makes us like them? Are they brave? Friendly? Shy?
- Is your protagonist an inventor? A warrior? Or just an ordinary kid going about their business, trying to stay out the way of the pointy-toothed walking trees that line the route to school?

≪
CREATE BOLD,
EXCITING
CHARACTERS,
SUCH AS THIS
IMPOSING FEMALE
WARRIOR.

## A THOUSAND FACES

Next, try to understand your protagonist's arc within the context of the narrative. Joseph Campbell's *The Hero with a Thousand Faces* lays out the building blocks of myths as they relate to character development. He described a three-part pattern as follows:

**1.** In the first part, the hero receives a call to adventure; he refuses it. He is then given supernatural aid and crosses a threshold, before falling into danger.

**2.** The second part begins with trials, followed by a meeting with a goddess. Then there is temptation, before reconciliation with the father. Finally, the hero acquires godlike powers. As a consequence of which, something enormously beneficial happens.

**3.** The third part concerns the hero's return, which begins with a refusal of the return; then a magical flight, rescue, crossing the return threshold, and becoming master. It ends with the hero living freely.

George Lucas, who had read Campbell's book, followed this pattern exactly in his first *Star Wars* movie, *Episode IV: A New Hope*, in which Luke Skywalker goes through all the stages of the hero's journey, and so achieves mythic status. Thinking about this structure can really help to bring your character out and allow your plot to go into warp drive.

You don't necessarily have to follow this pattern too closely, and it would be a very boring world if all books and movies did this. But it should help you to understand how the building blocks of a story are assembled: how plot and character work together intimately. Your character is affected by events, and isn't just blown about by fate, and what your character does has an important effect upon the world.

## TIPS AND TRICKS

When you're building your protagonist, try to imagine their ordinary world first. This is really important. Spend some time placing them within their daily lives: their bedroom, what they can see out of their windows, what they eat, what they do as a daily routine. Make a list of their favorite things and their dislikes.

Do this even with your villains and your minor characters, and you will be surprised at what you discover. Yes, that's the leader of the Altarian armies picking at his scabs. Yes, that's your gorgeous astral goddess gazing out across the turbulent Rivers of Muny'a, as she does every day in order to calibrate the levels of emotion in the world . . . and so on.

WATCH OUT FOR THIS
ANDROID HUNTER. . . .

## PROTAGONISTS

Think about the qualities you want your protagonist to have. Bravery, courage, valor, empathy. Sure, that's what they need. But they don't necessarily need to be boring do-gooders (in fact, that can be off-putting).

When we first meet the protagonist, the reader should feel drawn to them because of the situation they're in, as well as by their qualities and flaws. We need to be deeply invested in them, emotionally. You can do this by showing some action that's tender, or selfless, or kind; or demonstrate them standing up to a bully or righting some wrong.

Readers should be interested in your protagonist and want to see them win out the day. Whether that's by burning down the armies of Mo-ga-ru with a giant raygun or getting back to the old homestead on the watery fields of Uloth with the formula for saving kindly old Aunt Xendra from certain death, we still need to feel that we're reading about someone we'd like to hang out with.

## ANTAGONISTS

Usually, it's the protagonist whose life is disrupted by the movements or machinations of the antagonist. As a result, it will be your protagonist who suffers, and therefore gains our sympathy and empathy. Your protagonist will be the farmer on Jupiter's moons whose livelihood is threatened by the Galactic Megacorporation. Or the android going about her business when a new government takes over and wants all androids deactivated. Or perhaps a walking rabbit who enters a world where walking rabbits are hated. All she wants is carrots. But the world won't give her any.

For this reason, antagonists (or villains) can often spark a lot more energy. John Milton certainly discovered this when he wrote the epic poem *Paradise Lost*, in which Satan is close to becoming a tragic hero and is tortured by what he has to do. Adam's goodness and disobedience seem less important in comparison.

Good fiction thrives on contrasts. Think about your protagonist's character traits and see if you can contrast them with those of your antagonist. Your protagonist is brave—so make your antagonist braver, or cowardly. The antagonist is usually motivated by a need for power or control—consider what exactly it is that motivates them. Even the Terrifying Tentacular Tyrant of Marzovia has reasons for attacking the mining planets of Kazoom.

## TOO MANY CHARACTERS SPOIL THE BOOK

It's very tempting when composing sci-fi (or fantasy, for that matter) to fit in as many characters as possible.

You'll be imagining your protagonist, and then their families (or podmates, or whatever), and then their teachers, their enemies, the people they say hello to in the cyber-store, the guy who fixes hoverboards, and so on. This is always a bad thing, and it tends to happen a lot when writers are creating quest narratives.

My stellar advice to you is this: keep it small and keep it simple. While there is room for giant space operas with a million characters, when you're starting out, you only really need a few. This is partly to do with readability: when dealing with another world, or worlds, the reader must have something to hold on to, and this could be the fixed points of the characters.

Keep the canvas small, so you can draw your characters as boldly and as believably as possible.

# PROTAGONIST BUILDER

NAME:
.........................................................................

AGE:
.........................................................................

FAMILY:
.........................................................................
.........................................................................

PLACE OF BIRTH:
.........................................................................
.........................................................................

CURRENT HOME:
.........................................................................
.........................................................................

NEEDS:
.........................................................................
.........................................................................

WANTS:
.........................................................................
.........................................................................

HATES:
.........................................................................
.........................................................................

LOVES:
.........................................................................
.........................................................................

FAVORITE FOOD:
.........................................................................
.........................................................................

FAVORITE WEAPON:
.........................................................................
.........................................................................

ALLIES:
.........................................................................
.........................................................................

REASONS FOR ALLIANCE:
.........................................................................
.........................................................................

ENEMIES:
.........................................................................
.........................................................................

REASONS FOR RIVALRY:
.........................................................................
.........................................................................

# ANTAGONIST BUILDER

NAME:
...........................................................................

AGE:
...........................................................................

FAMILY:
...........................................................................
...........................................................................

PLACE OF BIRTH:
...........................................................................
...........................................................................

CURRENT HOME:
...........................................................................
...........................................................................

NEEDS:
...........................................................................
...........................................................................

WANTS:
...........................................................................
...........................................................................

HATES:
...........................................................................
...........................................................................

LOVES:
...........................................................................
...........................................................................

FAVORITE FOOD:
...........................................................................
...........................................................................

FAVORITE WEAPON:
...........................................................................
...........................................................................

ALLIES:
...........................................................................
...........................................................................

REASONS FOR ALLIANCE:
...........................................................................
...........................................................................

ENEMIES:
...........................................................................
...........................................................................

REASONS FOR RIVALRY:
...........................................................................
...........................................................................

# HUMANS AND HUMANOIDS

**AS WE'VE DUG** further into our past, we've discovered that our species of human *(Homo sapiens)* was not the only one. Recently, *Homo floresiensis*—a much smaller version of our own species—has been found.

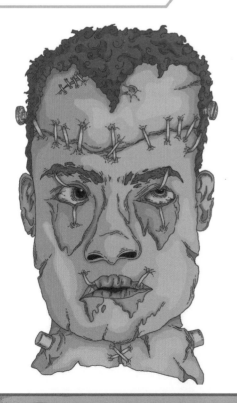

We also have the Neanderthals, of course, who lived on Earth at the same time as us, even interbreeding with us. This thought is enormously enticing—that there were once other beings like us, but not quite us, who walked alongside us for eons is fascinating.

Sci-fi gives you the opportunity to develop what it means to be a human. We mentioned Mary Shelley's *Frankenstein* in the introduction (see page 8) as being one of the first sci-fi novels, in which a human scientist builds another human out of body parts. And what it is to be human really remains one of the central questions of the genre.

Fantasy fiction already has a well-developed range of human-like beings: elves (tall, slender, impulsive), dwarves (short, stocky, like mining), goblins, orcs, hobbits, and so forth. With sci-fi, you can develop these ideas further. And not just by giving somebody green skin and red eyes. Here are some ideas to get you started:

**1.** Most UFO encounters deal with humanoid aliens—most famously, perhaps, the Greys. These have bulbous heads and enormous eyes, and they appear in many stories of people who believe they've been abducted by aliens. There's nothing quite so spooky as a lifeform that looks a bit like us, but just isn't, well, human. (See the next section, *Androids and Robots*, for more on this.)

**2.** A humanoid will most likely be upright, walk on two legs, and have opposable thumbs. Scientists have, in fact, theorized that intelligent life is likely to be humanoid, simply because when species evolve, sense organs develop at the front (thus resulting in a head) and then legs turn out to be useful for balancing. So, it really is possible.

**3.** Other sci-fi novels will give explanations for humanoid aliens—for example, the idea that humans were "seeded" across the galaxy, and allowed to increase, is a common one. It's also much easier for us to tell stories about humans, or human-like beings, simply because our minds can grasp their movements and actions more easily than, say, if we were dealing with people who are basically talking mushrooms.

**4.** You could also mix humans with animals—there are plenty of these in myth already, including centaurs and satyrs, and there's no reason why sci-fi can't deal with these too. In the Netflix series *Sweet Tooth*, for example, a boy has the horns and ears of a deer, caused by a virus sweeping the Earth.

YOU CAN DRAW ON MYTHOLOGY WHEN CREATING YOUR CHARACTERS— WHY NOT CREATE A PLANET FULL OF CREATURES CALLED CENTAURS THAT ARE PART HUMAN AND PART HORSE?

**5.** Could you imagine a world where humans have evolved differently from us? What if they had four arms? Or six eyes?

**6.** What if there was a terrible nuclear disaster, and the radioactive fallout made humans mutate into something entirely different in later generations?

Always remember the vulnerability of humans— and the power of humanity too, and its collective ability to both create and destroy.

# HUMANS AND HUMANOIDS: WRITING PROMPTS

**1. FIRST ENCOUNTER** Your protagonist is in the backyard playing basketball when a light appears in the sky. It gets closer and closer, until it appears to be a small spacecraft. It hovers about your protagonist, and a staircase unfolds from it.

**2. NEW ARRIVAL** A kid with silver hair and metallic eyes arrives at school . . . is she an alien? You have two days to find out.

**3. SPROUTING SCALES** Write about a character who wakes up with scales (as a fish), fur (as a bear), or a tail (as a cat).

**4. PARALLEL LIVES** A group of ancient Neanderthals is found in the freezing north. You're a scientist on an expedition to meet them. Describe your second week there in diary form.

**5. HUMANS ARE NOT . . .** Describe a humanoid being using six things that aren't human, and see what happens.

**6. LIVING AGAIN** Like the movie *Groundhog Day*, you must live the same day again and again. Pick either the day you lost a soccer game or the day you got angry with your sister. Put this on repeat. What did you learn? What would you change?

**7. ESSENCE OF HUMANITY** Asked by an alien to put 20 things in a capsule to represent humanity, what do you pick?

**8. BRAIN IN A JAR** Imagine a world where memories and personality can be uploaded to a computer. You awake knowing you're in the machine. Write a stream of consciousness (see page 57) response.

CHARACTER

**LITTLE MAN**
The remains of
*Homo floresiensis*,
a species of human
standing 3ft (1m) high,
were discovered in
Indonesia in 2004. The
original hobbits?

**LONG-LIVING**
The oldest human being in recorded history was Jeanne Calment—who lived to be 122 years old.

# ANDROIDS AND ROBOTS

**WE FIND ANDROIDS** so fascinating partly because they are uncanny. They look like us, talk like us, act like us; but they're not human. Or are they? This is one of the most fascinating questions posed by sci-fi.

The classic movie *Blade Runner* is an adaptation of Philip K. Dick's book *Do Androids Dream of Electric Sheep?*, in which a bounty hunter must track down several escaped androids. The book and the movie ask us to consider how we, as humans, are different from machines. Pádraig Kenny's book, *Tin*, sees Christopher as the only boy in a world full of mechanical robots. He's real because he is a human boy with a soul, though he's an orphan. When a secret is uncovered, he must go on a journey that will make him think about what it means to be alive. . . .

Cyborgs are a particular class of android: a human who has been fitted with technology in order to amplify particular abilities. They can be used to think about other issues too. Marissa Meyer's novel *Cinder* retells the story of Cinderella with a distinctly metallic twist. She's a cyborg, and is looked down on by her family, including, of course, her two sisters. But then she meets a handsome prince.

It's possible to have a lot of fun with robots because you can make them look like anything you want. Robots may have lost a little of their fascination in recent years, since we now have robot lawnmowers, robot vacuum cleaners, robot toys, and factories largely powered by robots. They are increasingly a part of everyday life and, perhaps, a little underwhelming. Yet it remains true that there's nothing more exciting than the idea of a giant robot. Ted Hughes' novel *The Iron Man*, for example, describes a touching friendship between a boy and a giant robot. Isaac Asimov's *I, Robot* is an important book that investigates precisely the effect of robotics on civilization. Asimov came up with the **Three Laws of Robotics**:

## FIRST LAW

A ROBOT MAY NOT INJURE A HUMAN BEING OR, THROUGH INACTION, ALLOW A HUMAN BEING TO COME TO HARM.

## SECOND LAW

A ROBOT MUST OBEY THE ORDERS GIVEN IT BY HUMAN BEINGS EXCEPT WHERE SUCH ORDERS WOULD CONFLICT WITH THE FIRST LAW.

## THIRD LAW

A ROBOT MUST PROTECT ITS OWN EXISTENCE AS LONG AS SUCH PROTECTION DOES NOT CONFLICT WITH THE FIRST OR SECOND LAWS.

THE THREE LAWS CAN LEAD TO POTENTIALLY SINISTER OR COUNTERINTUITIVE SIDES TO THE ADVANCE OF ROBOTS (OF COURSE). ASIMOV LATER ADDED A FOURTH LAW:

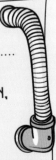

## ZEROTH LAW

A ROBOT MAY NOT HARM HUMANITY, OR, BY INACTION, ALLOW HUMANITY TO COME TO HARM.

Other questions can arise. If workers are all replaced by robots, then what will happen to the workers? Will it lead to mass unemployment and poverty? Or will it lead to a better future for all? What does it mean to be a human if a human does not need to work? There are other implications to allowing robots free rein over humans. For example, would you feel comfortable knowing that a self-driving car was deciding whether to protect you or the people on the sidewalk? Would you feel comfortable with a machine making any decision that affected your future?

The major issue with machines is that they are not accountable: the programmers, therefore, have huge amounts of power and responsibility, and how they program robots becomes all-important.

▶▶
DOES COUNTING ELECTRIC SHEEP MAKE ANDROIDS FALL ASLEEP?

# ANDROIDS AND ROBOTS: WRITING PROMPTS

**1. ROBOT HELP** It's 2034. Everyone has a house robot to do the housework. One day, you ask your robot to fetch you a lemonade from the fridge. And it refuses. Continue the scene.

**2. CYBORG SPECIAL** Describe visiting a surgeon to have two robotic superpowers put in—like increased sight or strength— and what it feels like to have them. Then imagine it all going wrong.

**3. BEND THE RULES** You diligently program androids. One day, you're tired and make a mistake. The next day, the android opens its eyes, and says: "Why am I here?" Fill in the next few minutes.

**4. CYBER ROMANCE** In the year 3024, robots can barely be distinguished from humans. Describe your protagonist's second date with a robot they have a crush on.

**5. KILLER BOTS** Assassin robots roam the world. Some rich people come to your village. Their defenses fail just as a robot assassin arrives. You can disable it with your stolen weapon. Describe what you do next.

**6. ROBOT LAWS** We learned about Asimov's Three Laws of Robotics. Can you think of any others?

**7. WRITE ABOUT ROBOTS** Think of six words related to robots and use these to write a story.

**8. ANDROID DREAMS . . .** Scribble down three things an android might dream about.

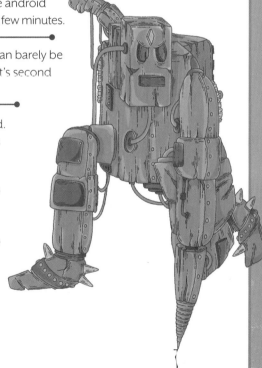

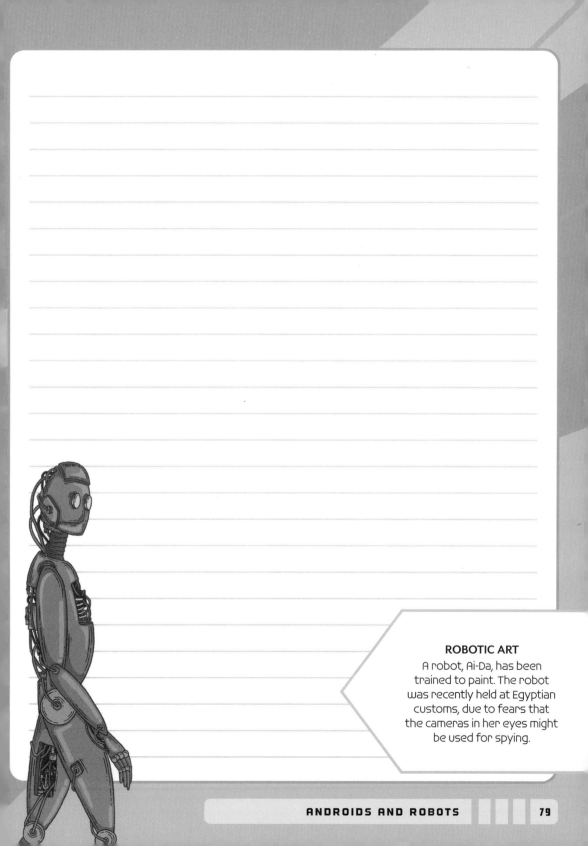

**ROBOTIC ART**

A robot, Ai-Da, has been trained to paint. The robot was recently held at Egyptian customs, due to fears that the cameras in her eyes might be used for spying.

**GODLY DEVICES**

In Homer's epic poem *The Iliad*, the Greek god of fire Hephaestus, who was a blacksmith and craftsman, is served by bronze handmaidens—like early robots!

# ALIENS!

Aliens that don't have a body and perhaps exist only as a shadow or thought create an intriguing vision. We tend to think of aliens as being blobby, tentacular things: essentially, as unhuman as possible. Sometimes they can be funny (think Jar Jar Binks in the *Star Wars* movies) or recognizably humanoid and cute, like E.T. in Stephen Spielberg's movie of the same name. More often than not, they are terrifying, monstrous creatures like the one in Ridley Scott's movie, *Alien*, all teeth, rage, and hunger.

Most sci-fi deals with aliens in some form or another. They help us to explore questions about evolution: how and why did we humans evolve in this particular form? Is such evolution possible on other planets?

Many writers draw on the idea that humans have colonized other planets over the centuries. Other writers imagine the kinds

"ARE YOU KIDDING? TAKE ME TO YOUR LEADER IS SO CLICHÉD!"

of aliens that might evolve on other planets. Are you really into biology? Then you could research the conditions on other planets, and work out what might be able to live on them. Is there heavier gravity? Then the creatures would be flatter. Or can the aliens there drink copper sulfate and breathe sulfur?

Some writers simply enjoy themselves when writing about aliens. Philip Reeve's *Cakes in*

*Space*, for example, not only has sentient, evil killer cakes and aliens that collect spoons, but also an alien known as the Nameless Horror—a shapeless, black mass, which actually turns out to be very friendly indeed.

It's extremely enjoyable to fill your new planets with gazillions of different kinds of species, from the tiniest crawling loofalah-worm, which survives only on magnesium, to the giant Malfasians who live on the tops of volcanic forests and eat bad poetry. You can construct a whole ecology, with each part fitting in to the next.

Think about what your aliens are there to do in terms of plot, character, and setting. How your protagonist interacts with them can be a way of exploring humanity. We love a good story in which humanity overcomes the enemy—the great success of the movie *Independence Day*, in which planet Earth is saved from an alien apocalypse by a fighter pilot, only goes to show this. If there is life in the universe, who says it's going to want to sit down, drink tea with us, and ask us about our Aunt Susan?

Despite all this, it can also be useful to think about different perspectives. Aliens don't always have to be the enemy. In Patrick Ness' Chaos Walking trilogy, the human colonists of a planet distrust the native species, the Spackle, believing that they caused the deaths of all the women in the colony. This is used as an excuse for war. Yet it turns out that the Spackle aren't quite the monsters they're meant to be. In Christopher Edge's *The Jamie Drake Equation*, the young hero picks up a signal from an alien.

Some writers have written about aliens on our own planet, coming from beneath the Earth's crust or popping over from different dimensions to say hello. They can come from anywhere, do anything. Go wild!

## FIVE FAMOUS ALIENS

▶▶ <u>E.T.</u> in *E.T. the Extra-Terrestrial*—a child helps a friendly alien return home.

▶▶ <u>The Martians</u> in *The War of the Worlds* by H.G. Wells—octopus-like creatures with beaks.

▶▶ <u>Hive Monks</u> in *Railhead* by Philip Reeve—insects that take the shape of a monk.

▶▶ <u>Formics</u> in *Ender's Game* by Orson Scott Card—a race of ant-like aliens that share a hive mind.

▶▶ <u>Thanos</u> in the *Avengers*—a warlord intent on wiping out half of all life in the universe.

A HIVE MONK—A SWARM OF INSECTS THAT CAN TAKE THE SHAPE OF A MONK—FROM PHILIP REEVE'S NOVEL *RAILHEAD*.

# ALIENS!: WRITING PROMPTS

**1. MIX AND MATCH** Write down the names of three animals—a giraffe, a frog, or a bird, for example. Then mix parts of them up to create your own alien.

**2. FOREST VISIT** You are an alien with three eyes. Imagine how this would affect your vision. Now, describe a visit to a forest on the alien's homeworld.

**3. BEST OF THE BESTIARY** On a distant planet, an alien professor is preparing a record of the animals. Write four entries for the scholar's book.

**4. PORTALS** A portal to another universe opens up your bedroom, and an alien falls out. The portal closes. Describe the alien, and how you could help it to adapt to life on Earth.

**5. POCKET PEST** A tiny, mischievous alien arrives in a woman's apartment. She has to carry it around in her bag. Describe what happens at her office next morning.

**6. ANIMAL INTELLIGENCE** A scientist is on an expedition to study a planet where there are primitive forms of life. She is following a herd of strange, cow-like animals. One day, she starts to communicate with them. Write her log.

**7. FREE WRITING** Clear your mind, and then speed-write for 15 minutes about an encounter with an alien, using the following words once each: mustard, tree, tentacle, piano, night.

**8. ALIENS AT HOME** Write a short piece from the perspective of an alien child, who's being transferred to a school on Earth.

PANSPERMIA
The theory that
life was spread in
the universe by
meteorites.

CHARACTER

Scientists in 2020 thought they might have found evidence of bacterial life forms in the atmosphere of Venus . . . the Venusians!

# CHAPTER 3

# PLOT

THE SETTING FOR YOUR WORLD—THE STRANGE AND GLORIOUS LANDSCAPES YOU CREATE—IS THE MOST IMPORTANT ASPECT OF YOUR SCI-FI STORY AND IS WHAT READERS WILL PROBABLY REMEMBER MOST. YOUR CHARACTERS ARE ALSO VERY IMPORTANT. BUT SO TOO IS THE PLOT. READ ON TO FIND OUT WHY.

**YOUR PLOT IS CRUCIAL.** It's closely linked to the setting and the characters (you'll discover this as you begin to write sci-fi). If you spend a lot of time thinking about your setting, then your characters will be more believable. This will then give you the beginnings of a plot. If you start with a plot, you will more than likely find yourself getting stuck.

If you start with a world or an idea—for example, a boy who is given a bionic eye or a girl who stumbles upon the secret of space travel—you'll find that the plot suggests itself. That bionic eye will have problems. The secret of space travel will be wanted by other people.

Be in no doubt—what most readers want when they read a sci-fi story is a plot that pulls you in as powerfully as a tractor beam, and drags you through all the way until the end.

## KEEP IT SIMPLE . . . TO START WITH

There is a tendency with sci-fi to think on the grand, galactic scale when it comes to plot. Yes, you want seven different plots set in 18 different planets with a cast of thousands, ranging from the Gramboolian Gorgosan Spider King to the many-legged, multidimensional beings that inhabit the Galactic Web.

However, it's always the case that if you start big, you'll get confused, and your reader will get confused as well. Don't overcomplicate things. You may be tempted, as you write, simply to go along and throw in everything that you think of. For example: "There was a boy, and he went to a planet which was made of ice, and then he met a giant talking polar bear, and then there was a giant ray gun and then everything exploded!" is a pretty good summary of the suggestions I might get when doing workshops. Yes, the planet made of ice is good; yes, the giant polar bear is good, but, whoa, where did the giant ray gun come from? And why does everything have to explode?

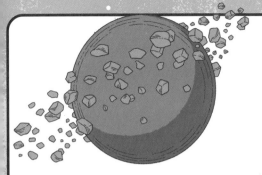

There are many ways of thinking about plot. The novelist John Gardner said there were only two plots: a person goes on a journey or a stranger comes to town. The writer Patricia Duncker agrees, saying there are basically only two types of plot: siege narratives or quest narratives. Either you're being attacked by an enemy or going out in search of something.

Think carefully about your characters and your setting. Is your lovely little utopian world where ice cream grows on trees at risk of being taken over by an evil corporation that only wants to harvest the ice cream for its own nefarious usages? Then there will need to be a character (the protagonist) who stands up to the corporation and a series of events that leads to a confrontation with that corporation. The resolution will then either be that the corporation backs off and leaves the ice-cream planet to its own devices (yay!), or the corporation conquers the planet and forces everyone into financial servitude for eternity (boo!). Everything has to be logical, and everything has to be linked together.

## SEVEN BASIC PLOTS?

The writer Christopher Booker has suggested that there are actually seven basic plots. People argue about this all the time. Even so, it can be quite useful to think about Booker's categories in relation to your own sci-fi. When you're starting to plan your work, you can use one of these as a hook to hang your own on. Plot is all about movement toward an ending: events have beginnings and middles and endings, and they also have consequences.

BOOKER'S SEVEN BASIC PLOTS:

**1.** Overcoming the Monster: This is a classic sci-fi plot—for example, in *The Last Kids on Earth* by Max Brallier, a bunch of kids defend their treehouse from zombies and monsters.

**2.** Rags to Riches: Less often found, but still quite powerful. A good example is *Ready Player One* by Ernest Cline, which sees a poor kid win a fortune in a virtual reality game.

**3.** Quest: More often than not found in fantasy, but still useful in sci-fi—for example, in *The Many Worlds of Albie Bright* by Christopher Edge, a young boy travels through many universes in a quest for one in which his mother is still alive.

**4.** Voyage and Return: This provides a good sci-fi framework, allowing you to contrast the going out and coming back. H.G. Wells' *The Time Machine* uses this structure through time.

**5.** Tragedy: Most books for kids don't use this tragic arc. But you could think of something along the lines of Lemony Snicket's series, *A Series of Unfortunate Events*, in which the children's adventures usually end in disaster.

**6.** Comedy: This doesn't mean it has to be laugh-out-loud funny. It means that the plot has a happy ending. Douglas Adams' *The Hitchhiker's Guide to the Galaxy* is hilarious and does (eventually) have a happy ending.

**7.** Rebirth: Usually to do with the spiritual rebirth of a character, such as Scrooge in Dickens' *A Christmas Carol*. In other words, a character will start off in a bad way, then end up reformed. The TV series *Doctor Who* had a Christmas special that retold the Dickens' story, but with a miser (a person reluctant to spend money) called Old Kazran—the Doctor meddles with his timeline in order to teach him how to love.

The great thing about sci-fi is that you can use any classic plot structure (that's in the public domain, obviously) and transfer it to another planet or another time. For example, think about setting William Shakespeare's play *Macbeth* on Pluto. (Incidentally, the Shakespeare scholar A.D. Nuttall claimed Shakespeare invented science fiction and that *The Tempest* is a play that has been retold many times within the genre—the movie *Forbidden Planet*, for example, is based on it.) Or try setting Homer's *The Odyssey* in the Andromeda Galaxy. Or perhaps Mary Shelley's *Frankenstein* on a giant spaceship. Or try Herman Melville's *Moby Dick*, but with a great white spacewhale. (Spacewhales, again, huh? Always with the spacewhales!) Or Nathaniel Hawthorne's *The Scarlet Letter* on a new colony planet thousands of years into the future.

## BUILDING BLOCKS

Your plot needs to be paced out evenly: if too many things happen in the first few pages, and then not very much happens throughout the middle, your reader will go and find a different story to read.

To pace your plot, you need a solid structure: in other words, the order in which your story is told. To start with, I would recommend sticking to a chronological structure. (You can, of course, experiment with this, using flashbacks or flashforwards.)

One major problem I see in sci-fi manuscripts is too much information being crammed at the begining because it is information they think their reader will need in the following chapters. Complex new worlds require a lot of explanation, but the reader doesn't necessarily want to be involved in a lot of backstory before the main action starts.

We want to be in the world as if it has always been there, and the plot should seem like a natural extension of an event that happens in that world (or to it, if it's coming from somewhere else.)

## CRUCIAL POINTS

▷ What happens before your story? Think about what life was like in the days and weeks before the story begins. We call this the "status quo"—normal life, before it's changed.

▷ The disrupting event is often called the inciting incident. This could be, for example, the release of a deadly virus from a laboratory. Or it could be as simple as an explorer arriving in a new world and setting up camp.

WHAT A GREAT PLACE TO WRITE SCI-FI—
YOU'RE SURROUNDED BY INSPIRATION.

▷ The middle is the main bulk of the novel, and this will be an extension of the inciting incident, leading to a chain of events that are usually centered on conflict. The protagonist will learn new things that point the way toward a solution. This can take the form of clues, or meetings, or information given in other ways. If you choose the deadly virus example, then it will cause chaos; your protagonist will evade it somehow, and perhaps join up with a group of others who have so far escaped.

▷ The ending will be a resolution of the events. For example, the deadly plague is contained

or beaten. This needs to happen through the logical steps of the story, not by chance. Similarly, the terrifying, monstrous alien is killed or returned to its homeworld. Or the ship reaches its destination, or the lost voyager comes home.

The ending will tend to be a happy one, or at least upbeat or resolved. Obviously, this isn't always the case, especially with dystopian fiction.

A finely engineered plot will help power your sci-fi all the way to the stars. And beyond. Who knows, you might find readers on Mars.

# GOING BOLDLY: VOYAGES

**THE SCI-FI GENRE** is the perfect vehicle for writing about exciting voyages and adventures into the unknown, allowing you to indulge your imagination with some wild and wonderful modes of transport.

Sci-fi stories lend themselves particularly well to voyages: ever since the Argonauts sailed for Colchis to gain the Golden Fleece or Odysseus came back from Troy to find his kingdom overrun, the fantastical voyage has been a mainstay of fiction. With sci-fi in particular, many opportunities present themselves. On our own planet, journeys to the most extreme parts of the globe, as well as into the ocean depths and the center of the Earth itself, provide immensely fertile ground for journeys. Our own bodies also offer up possibilities, such as a technology that can shrink us and send us in to have a poke around somewhere that's usually inaccessible. For example, you could miniaturize yourself and go into someone's body to help fight a disease. And then there are the limitless infinities of space and beyond. Take a look at the two examples below:

▷ In Madeleine L'Engle's *A Wrinkle in Time*, the three heroes travel through the universe using a mysterious object called a tesseract.

▷ In *George's Secret Key to the Universe* by Lucy and Stephen Hawking, Cosmos is able to draw windows and doors that can be used as portals to head into outer space. It's also full of scientific information.

Think about how you feel as you travel. The excitement of preparing your suitcases and the anticipation of waiting for the car or plane. The boredom of travel. The relief of arriving. Think about how each of these things would affect a character.

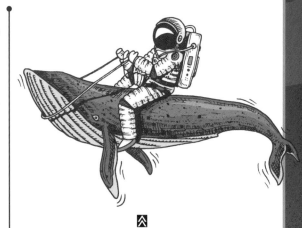

"HI-HO, SILVER!"
ADD A SCI-FI TWIST TO STORIES YOU KNOW BY CHANGING THE SPECIES AND SETTING. HERE WE HAVE AN ASTRONAUT RIDING A WHALE, INSTEAD OF JOHN REID RIDING "SILVER," THE HORSE FROM *THE LONE RANGER*.

The series of sci-fi novels The Long Earth Sequence by Terry Pratchett and Stephen Baxter uses the idea of parallel universes: in other words, alongside our Earth are millions of other ones that can be reached by a simple process known as Stepping.

Your journey should include the details of something real: in *The Odyssey*, for example, Homer spends a lot of time explaining how the ship works, in spite of Odysseus' exciting encounters with marvelous beings and creatures.

We should feel your characters' emotions as they make their way from one place to another: their hopes and dreams, their frustrations when these are denied. Reading accounts of real voyages can help with this: Read up on Arnelia Earhart, the first female aviator to fly across the Atlantic, or the Viking, Leif Erikson, who traveled with his 35-man crew to see if there was land beyond Greenland. Often, it's

the tiny details that make things come alive. Let's take an example from history. During the French Revolution, King Louis XVI of France and his family managed to escape from Versailles in 1791, but they were caught and forced to make a long coach journey back to Paris. Historians have often wondered how he and his children dealt with their needs on the journey. The answer is that the king helped his son to pee into a silver bottle. The journey should follow a simple structure. Getting ready. Finding the transport. The journey itself. Problems along the way. Arrival. The prompts in this section (although they refer to different stories) will, taken by themselves, help you to structure a whole narrative.

Just remember to bring a drink to keep you going on your journey. And also pack some warm underwear, just in case. Even astronauts need it.

# VOYAGES: WRITING PROMPTS

**1. PREPARATION** Write down a list of the things a deep-sea diver and explorer would need to reach the farthest depths of the ocean. Describe the day when all the necessary items for the journey have been found, except one.

**2. SETTING OUT** An astronaut is leaving home for the first time to undergo an important voyage to a distant star. Focus on the details: what favorite objects, foods, and so on should be left behind?

**3. THE LONG VOYAGE** Plan an itinerary for a spaceship's journey from one of the moons of Jupiter to a different galaxy. Are there any stops and dangers along the way?

**4. THE FIRST SETBACK** A cruising starship bearing several hundred passengers to a different planet meets an unexpected danger. Write about what happens next.

**5. THE TEMPTATION** On a long and important journey across a desert planet, your protagonist meets a group of luxury-loving travelers who offer a life of ease and pleasure. What happens next?

**6. THE FINAL SETBACK** After a long war in the colonies of Mars, a soldier takes 20 years to travel home. Just as the soldier reaches the shuttle that will return him to Earth, he meets a final challenge. Describe his reaction.

**7. ARRIVAL** A scientist has traveled for years carrying a secret key. She is now within sight of her home. But, just as she reaches the path that leads up to the front door, she sees an enemy inside. What does she do?

**8. RESTLESSNESS** An explorer has returned home from her final mission. Describe her meeting with her partner and children, showing how, while she's happy to be at home, she's also feeling restless and unsure about staying in one place. Focus on physical details.

**KEY WORD**

ODYSSEY

Taken from Homer's epic poem *The Odyssey*, this word can be used to describe any long, difficult journey.

## KEY WORDS

ALCUBIERRE DRIVE
A theoretical concept for the creation of a spaceship that does not move, but the space around it does. This could allow ships to travel faster than the speed of light.

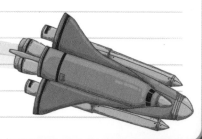

PLOT

**INTO THE UNKNOWN**
The space probe *Voyager 1* is
the first human-made object to
enter interstellar space.

# INVASIONS

**THIS IS POSSIBLY** one of the most popular categories in the sci-fi genre. Everyone is sitting around minding their own business, arguing with their siblings or playing a computer game, when—kaboom!—Earth is invaded by aliens, terrible complications ensue, and the hero has to save the day.

An invasion story is a simple one. Write it well, and you will have an excellent story. Dozens of movies and novels use this idea—most notably the movie *Independence Day*, in which the White House is blown up by invading aliens. There's a lot of bang and bluster in this movie. But the invasion can be done more subtly, such as in the movie *The Faculty,* in which a high school becomes the setting for an invasion of alien parasites that disappear into the bodies of the teachers. The teen students have to find the aliens' weak point before disaster occurs.

Perhaps the most haunting alien invasion movie is *The Invasion of the Body Snatchers*, in which plant-like aliens copy humans and then destroy them. The 1978 version, which stars

Donald Sutherland, is one of the best sci-fi movies of all time. The final scene, in which Sutherland's character realizes that he's pretty much the only human left, is terrifying. I highly recommend it. But watch it with friends or your guardians. And *MAKE SURE THEY ARE NOT SECRETLY GIANT PLANTS* .

Your first decision, then, is whether you want to do something on a grand scale: with terrifying aliens who land and all but destroy the world. H. G. Wells' novel *The War of the Worlds* is a great example of this and is all the more frightening because it is set in the counties around London. When a monster's in a small town, they are much more threatening— it brings the threat closer to home and you might not receive the same aid from authorities as you would in New York. That's the first point: ground your invasion in the real and everyday lives of your characters.

There's a lovely comic novel by Adam Rex called *The True Meaning of Smekday*, in which heroine Gratuity tells the story of an alien invasion. Her mom's abducted, and a race of aliens called the Boov arrive—on Christmas Day. And they rename Christmas "Smekday." One of the aliens becomes friends with Gratuity—and calls himself J.Lo.

*Bloom*, by Kenneth Oppel, is a suspenseful story that reinterprets *Invasion of the Body Snatchers*. Here, three children watch as their world is taken over by giant alien plants that eat people. Told you to watch out for those plants!

You could also do something on a smaller scale. Nicholas Fisk's classic novel *Trillions* begins in a small English village with a sudden invasion of lots—well, trillions—of tiny crystals, which then shift themselves to create different shapes. Are they a threat, or are they benevolent? The book creates a wonderfully tense atmosphere as the child heroes attempt to work this out.

One of the main things that alien invasion stories do is force us to think about what's important in our lives. What could we live with and what could we do without? What would you save if you saw a giant spaceship hovering above your house?

And, of course, there's also the fun involved in thinking about what kinds of aliens could descend and land on Earth.

# INVASIONS: WRITING PROMPTS

**1. FIRST CONTACT** You are a scientist in a research facility monitoring radio waves. One day, you find and decode a message from an alien race. It warns of an invasion. Write a short piece in which the scientist ponders what to do with the message.

**2. STRANGE BEHAVIOR** A student is in her school canteen when she notices that one of her friends is behaving oddly. Later, she sees the same friend putting something moving into the school bully's ear. Describe the scene, using the first person.

**3. MOMENT OF WEAKNESS** A city has been overtaken by octopus-like aliens. You have two days to find their weakness before the whole country is overrun. Describe the moment you find the solution. Use the words: lemonade, diamond, nocturnal.

**4. TRAPPED!** An isolated farmhouse is the only outpost where three people have gathered to hide out from an invasion. You are one of these people. One morning, you wake up and see an alien scout has arrived. Describe the battle that follows, using the first person.

**5. SPACE INVADERS** Write a scene at alien high command involving a discussion about why the Earth is the target for invasion. One of the soldiers is against the attack.

**6. THE RESISTANCE** It's been a year since the Earth was taken over by humanoid aliens. Humans are totally subjugated. You are invited to join a resistance cell. Describe the moment you are first contacted to do this.

**7. PEACE, MAN** An alien spaceship arrives, bearing several hundred humanoid aliens. But its passengers only want one thing: somewhere to live peacefully. Their own planet is dying. Describe a scene showing how they might be received by a small city.

**8. ATTACK!** A spaceship full of humans is on its way to attack another planet, where humans are considered aliens. Write a few paragraphs from the point of view of one of the home planet's inhabitants.

**EASY MISTAKE TO MAKE**
Most UFO/ UAP reports turn out to be easily explained phenomena, such as the object that crashed in Roswell, New Mexico. It was, in fact, a weather balloon.

### RUN FOR THE HILLS
In 1938, Orson Welles' adaptation of H. G. Wells' *The War of the Worlds* was broadcast live. It reportedly caused panic among listeners because they thought it was really happening.

# LASERS AND SPACE BATTLES

WE THINK OF LASERS WHEN WE IMAGINE SPACE BATTLES: SHOTS OF LIGHT, BOUNCING OFF SHIPS AND CAUSING MASSIVE EXPLOSIONS. Which is silly, really, as lasers are just light, and could do about as much damage as a damp washcloth.

You need think about how your armory of weapons works and what each of them can do within the laws of physics. You can do this in great detail, as for invasions (see page 102), or just sketch in something that has a ring of plausibility. You can go down the hard sci-fi route, where equipment is governed according to very strict scientific or mathematical rules, or you can be more relaxed with soft sci-fi that focuses more on the characters and the adventure than it does on the technology. Either way, you still have to think about the same things.

There's no doubt about it, space battles are spectacular. The sheer, vast scale of spaceships, or the damage a falling ship can do to a planet, makes the stakes incredibly high on both a personal and wider level. Such battles give novels a spectacular climax (see page 117), particularly if readers are invested in the outcome for specific characters. Orson Scott Card's *Ender's Game*

contains some awesome space battles: the story follows a boy who's being trained for war in space.

You could try to write some epic space battles. Think about an evil empire, controlling all in its path. A band of rebels must save the universe. How would they go about it? Think about a war between men and machines: how would humans defend their planet from a cyborg attack? How would you deal with a war between artificial intelligences and humans? Always look for the weaknesses. And, it goes without saying, your reader will always root for the little guy.

And don't underestimate the power of the duel: think of the epic light-saber fights in the

*Star Wars* movies. We need someone to root for, and this needs to be linked to the overall plot structure.

When planning your space battle, first think about your characters. You need someone to follow through the battle. Is your character a captain, in control of everything? Or a soldier, following orders? The spaceship itself can have a powerful presence—think of Star Trek's *USS Enterprise*. If you name your ship, the reader will be able to follow the battle more easily.

Then think about the setting. Where is the battle taking place? Is it in deep space or above a planet? There are, of course, problems with distance in space: you want the ships to meet up close and personal, rather than hurl missiles at each other from millions of miles away.

Readers also appreciate it when you consider tactics. Who is fighting what, and why? What forces does the protagonist's side have? And the opposition's? Think of famous battles in history: we remember the fall of the 300 Spartans at Thermopylae in 470 BCE because of the terrible odds stacked against them. What are the advantages and disadvantages for both sides? And does either side have any tricks up their sleeves? Reading some military history can be helpful here.

And remember: when ships explode or get damaged, it's the human cost that makes the impact count. Explosions by themselves are simply fireworks.

# SPACE BATTLES: WRITING PROMPTS

**1. CRASH, BANG, BOOM** Come up with as many sound words as you can in 30 seconds. Now write a paragraph about a space battle using five of them.

**2. BATTLE PLANS** You're in command of a fleet of warships attacking a larger ship. Write a message containing orders for your soldiers. Make the orders simple.

**3. A SOLDIER'S LIFE FOR ME** On the war planet of Mars, soldiers are trained to fight from birth. Describe a day in the life of a young boy or girl at war school.

**4. PANORAMIC VIEW** The Empress of the Galaxy watches a space battle from her viewing platform. Her forces are being attacked by pirates. Describe what she sees.

**5. DECISIONS, DECISIONS** A general is in charge of a fleet of starships. They are under attack. He knows that if he sacrifices two of his ships, the others will survive. What does he do? Write a story in which he makes his decision.

**6. SPACE SPIDERS** Yes, here they are again, but I simply couldn't resist. Describe a climactic stage in a battle between two armies of warring space spiders. Write from the point of view of one of the soldier spiders.

**7. FEELING FEARFUL** A soldier is on her first trip on what is meant to be a routine inspection of an asteroid. But the ship is buzzed by an enemy. Focus on her emotional state and write a short paragraph. Use sensory detail.

**8. EPIC BATTLE** OK, now you can go crazy. Do what you want: describe the biggest space battle you can imagine and have always wanted to write about. Just make sure to keep a protagonist in mind. Go for it!

## KEY WORDS
DOOMSDAY DEVICE
A theoretical weapon,
capable of taking out
an entire planet.

**REALITY BITES**

A real space battle probably wouldn't involve a crewed ship at all, but vehicles controlled from the ground instead like modern-day drones.

**KEY WORD**

CLIMAX

Usually nearing the end of the book, at the highest point of interest in a story.

# VIRTUAL REALITY

**WE LIVE IN AN EXTRAORDINARY UNIVERSE**, and we are learning more about it with every day that passes.

⟫ TECHNOLOGICAL ADVANCES MEAN YOU CAN NOW TUNE INTO A VIRTUAL WORLD AND SEE BEYOND THE STARS.

Each day, our senses provide us with so much wonderful information about our world: we can see, hear, smell, touch, and taste; these sensations feed into our minds and our emotions. They also give us pleasure, pain, and everything in between. Stand in a forest and breathe in the clear air or watch the busy streets in a city and marvel at the ways of humanity.

So, why would anybody want to go into a virtual world where none of these things exist and everything is sterile—and is conceived by the mind of another person? And what are the dangers of building virtual worlds that mimic our own and offer easier ways to live, so much so that people start to want to stay in them?

The relevance of these questions is coming ever closer, as technologies gain more and more power. At the moment, VR tech is pretty basic—nobody would be fooled into thinking they were *really* in a different place. But for how much longer will this be the case? And what will happen to our sense of ourselves and the world around us when this happens? There are many troubling questions to consider: is theft in the virtual world the same as in the real one?

In *Trapped in a Video Game* by Dustin Brady, Jesse gets—well, you can guess from the title—stuck inside a video game, and has to work out how to escape. In the YA world, Jason Segel's *Otherworld* tells of a terrifying future where virtual reality is an almost perfect version of our own. Players become dangerously addicted.

*Girl Gone Viral* by Arvin Ahmadi is about a 17-year-old girl, Opal, who creates virtual worlds. When the world's biggest virtual reality platform starts a competition, she discovers some things about her father that propel her into dangerous situations.

If your characters are inside a virtual world, they should still be able to hear, smell, and touch. Make sure they're using their senses. Otherwise you'll lose your reader.

If you can make use of the uncanny (the strange, mysterious, and hard to explain) that is all to the good too. You may have heard of the Uncanny Valley—this is a term used to describe the relationship between the appearance of a human avatar (see page 123) or robot and our emotional response to it. The possibilities opened up by virtual worlds are endlessly uncanny, and also provoke several interesting questions. Would you, for example, like to upload images of your relatives, so that you could enjoy a virtual relationship with them when they die? And how would you feel about the same thing happening to you? There's lots to consider in a virtual world.

# VIRTUAL REALITY: WRITING PROMPTS

**1. IT'S ALL UNREAL** Our world is an illusion. Our real bodies are elsewhere. Describe the moment a character discovers this.

**2. PULLING THE PLUG** All virtual reality games are mysteriously stopped one day. Describe how an addicted player comes out into the real world. Focus on the senses.

**3. ODD ONE OUT** In a virtual world, a character realizes that they are the only real person. Write an entry in log form.

**4. VIRTUAL LOVE** Two players of a massive online role-playing game fall in love with each other. But in real life, they are enemies. Describe the moment they realize this is the case in the real world.

**5. BOUND IN A NUTSHELL** A criminal has committed a virtual crime by stealing a precious artifact and is cast into a virtual prison. Describe Day 117.

**6. ETERNAL LIFE** Humans can download their brains onto a virtual system. Write a letter to a friend from someone who doesn't want to do this.

**7. VIRTUAL TO REAL** An enemy that was created in virtual space finds a way of downloading itself into a real body and begins to terrorize a town. Describe what happens next.

**REALITY AS HOLOGRAM**
Some philosophers argue that this world is actually a virtual world, created by a future civilization.

## KEY WORD
METAVERSE
Coined by Neal Stephenson in *Snow Crash*, this word is used to describe a virtual reality version of the Internet.

PLOT

# ALTERNATE HISTORIES

**BEAR WITH ME FOR A MOMENT** and follow me backward, deep into the murky mists of time, to what used to be called the Dark Ages.

Here we are in the 6th century CE. The Visigothic chief Alaric II is fighting the Battle of Vouillé against the Frankish Clovis. This is not a battle you'll have learned about in school, or even heard of in popular fiction or history. But it is important: representing a turning point in world history. Alaric lost and Clovis won, so history ran its course and we are where we are today.

However, if Alaric had won, then it's entirely possible that the Visigoths would have been in charge of Iberia (modern Spain) and Gaul (modern France); that the Visigoths would have ruled over most of Europe; that the Roman Catholic Church would have pretty much disappeared; and that France would not exist.

As the historian Norman Davies says in his account of the matter: "Nothing is inevitable. Nothing is perfectly predictable."

I've always been fascinated by these turning points in history, and sci-fi offers a brilliant way to consider them. You could take almost any significant point in history and think about how things might have turned out differently. Could you imagine a different world history in which Japan and Germany had won the Second World War, and America was under Nazi control? The Amazon Prime series *The Man in the High Castle* shows this, and is based on a novel of the same name by Philip K. Dick. How about a world with no Black Death devastating the populations of Europe? Or one in which the Roman Empire never ended? Or one where British forces beat President Andrew Jackson at the Battle of New Orleans? Or one where Abraham Lincoln wasn't assassinated? Or John F. Kennedy? All these ideas look at huge, historical shifts which had many causes. To do the same, you have to conduct plenty of research into the area you're examining. Approach this, first and foremost, as if you're writing a piece of historical fiction.

When writing alternate histories, it can also be helpful to think about tiny things that have enormous and far-reaching consequences. For instance, one of my favorite short stories as a boy was Ray Bradbury's "A Sound of Thunder." This is set in a future when time travel is possible: people are allowed to go back in time to hunt dinosaurs, for example, but they aren't allowed to change anything. One of the characters steps on a butterfly in the past and then returns to the present to find that the timeline has changed drastically, with a fascist candidate winning an election.

It's also fun to consider changes in our own lives, using the parallel universe concept (that many slightly different universes exist alongside ours). What if you didn't win that prize, or catch that train, or meet that teacher? How would your life have changed? The movie *Sliding Doors* shows a life that hinges on one tiny moment with fascinating results. And the *Back to the Future* movies also play with the concept of different timelines affecting people's lives.

Just be careful here. If you go back in time, don't accidentally kill your own grandparent. If you do, then you won't ever be born, which means you won't ever have gone back to kill your grandparent. This means that he'll still be alive and so you will be born, which means. . . .

# ALTERNATE HISTORIES: WRITING PROMPTS

**1. FLOW CHART** Take an ordinary student on an ordinary day. Build two flow charts: one in which everything the student does goes right that day, then one in which it doesn't. Now write out both versions.

**2. IN THE BEGINNING . . .** Describe an Earth on which the dinosaurs never became extinct. Did humans evolve?

**3. A POINT IN TIME** You discover a door that sends you back into the past. You use this as an opportunity to check out some questions in a test. When you return to the present, you ace the test, but something else terrible happens. Describe the moment when you realize what you've done.

**4. HORRIBLE HISTORIES** Choose one of the following (or your own): the Revolutionary War; the invasion of England by William of Normandy; or the fall of the Roman Empire. Now imagine what would happen if the outcome were different. Jot down a few ideas, then draw up a newspaper report.

**6. MEDDLERS** There is a team of covert operatives who exist to go back in time and change things for the better. One member has just joined. Describe their headquarters.

**5. ON THE WRONG SIDE** One morning, everything is subtly different—there's a different president and a different language. Nobody else seems to have noticed anything. Describe your day in diary form.

**7. SAVING YOURSELF** A portal opens into a world where a much more successful version of you lives. Describe what you decide to do?

**RUNNING BACKWARD?**
Scientists think they
have found evidence
of an alternate mirror
world, thanks to an
experiment in Antarctica
with a giant balloon,
where time runs
backward. . . .

**KEY WORD**

ANACHRONOUS

Not suitable for the time period. For example, a character wearing a watch in a medieval era.

**KEY WORDS**
FERMI PARADOX
If time travel were possible, then ask yourself: where are all the visitors from the future?

## OPENING UP THE WORLD

In around 1440, the printing press was invented by Johannes Gutenberg, allowing books to be rapidly copied and transported. It's a key point in world history.

PLOT

1914 . . .
The First World War is often seen as a vital turning point in modern history. Consider what would have happened had the Archduke Franz Ferdinand not been assassinated in 1914.

# CHAPTER 4

# DIALOGUE

YOU PROBABLY SPEND A LOT OF YOUR TIME TALKING. YOU ALSO PROBABLY SPEND A LOT OF YOUR TIME LISTENING TO OTHER PEOPLE TALK, PARTICULARLY WHEN YOU'RE WATCHING YOUR FAVORITE SHOWS, OR LISTENING TO THE RADIO, OR WHEN YOU'RE WITH YOUR FRIENDS, OR AT SCHOOL, OR WITH YOUR FAMILY.

Dialogue is an important part of fiction, but it's not the only part. There's a kind of general belief in creative writing that dialogue makes the reading experience snappier and even easier. It doesn't. Let me kill that one, right there.

What you have to remember is that storytelling is, first and foremost, a narrative form: that you're *telling* a story. Quite often, I'll see long sections of dialogue in manuscripts, and I always suggest my students rewrite parts of their stories without any dialogue at all. The results are nearly always better.

The strange thing about dialogue on the page is that it's different from how people speak in real life, and yet it still has to sound as if it has been spoken naturally. (It's also different from dialogue on screen, which often has to serve a plot function.)

If you were to record a quick conversation between a couple of friends, then it might go something like this:

**Zane:** "Oh hey, I like your backpack."
**Nisha:** "Hey!"
**Zane:** "Hey! So how's it going?"

**Nisha:** "Like . . . hang on . . . . My backpack is pretty cool, isn't it. Hey, leave it alone!"
**Zane:** "I've been asking Mom to get me one for like ages. Oh hey, Zach!"
**Nisha:** "I'm so over this class. Have you done the school assignment?"

You can see that it's a bit random, that the questions asked aren't immediately answered, that there are repetitions, and that the subject is changed for no reason. This is because, in real life, our conversations rely a lot on nonverbal cues, and also on the previous relationships and knowledge of the speakers involved.

Put that into fiction, though, and it will be flat and dull on the page. There may be space for realistic, non-sequitur-filled dialogue in experimental theater and fiction (a response that does not follow the conversation, like replying with, "I'm fine" when you were asked about the weather), but you'll find it doesn't work so well for most readers.

# WHAT DOES DIALOGUE DO?

There are three main things that dialogue should do, as follows:

**1.** Tell the reader about character. How your protagonist talks to someone gives us a lot of information. You could have one astronaut whose personality is, ahem, out of this world, and the other who's a bit more down to earth. (I'm here all night, people.) So they would talk differently—one more enthusiastically, the other in shorter, more blunt sentences.

**2.** Tell the reader about plot. It's a tricky one, this, as you can't use dialogue to impart too much information. If your characters are telling each other things they already know, then it's a sure sign that there is too much dialogue. But sometimes it's necessary. Keep an eye out, though, for too much exposition. (Exposition is when you insert background information into the story, often at the beginning.)

**3.** Create atmosphere and lighten moments of tension. Here, dialogue is particularly good for adding humor to the story or for rounding off a scene with an ironic comment.

≫
HERE'S THAT ANDROID HUNTER
AGAIN. BE CAREFUL!

## PROBLEMS WITH SCI-FI

With sci-fi, the dialogue can seem particularly difficult, as we have to imagine what people might talk like in the future, or on other planets. Although you don't necessarily want people to sound like they do today, you do want your readers to be able to understand and empathize with what they're saying.

## MODULATE! MODULATE!

Dialogue should also modulate: firstly, depending on whom the character is addressing. Your child protagonist will shift style between talking to parents, teachers, and friends, just as you do. You probably speak more formally to a teacher or someone in authority than you do to a friend. This opens up all sorts of possibilities in sci-fi: how, for example, would a child talk to a robot?

You can also use dialogue (or a lack of it) to show shifts in emotion. One key thing to grasp is the value of silence: "She said nothing" can be a very effective way of showing a crucial moment and allowing the reader to fill in the gaps.

Body language is just as important as what people say. Remember that you can always write: "He shrugged" instead of "'I don't understand,' he said."

## LANGUAGE, LANGUAGE

Another issue with dialogue in sci-fi is that you'll be dealing with lots of other planets. And, of course, if these planets existed in real life, then the inhabitants would be speaking entirely different languages—if they even speak at all. The aliens in the recent movie *Arrival* (2016) communicate entirely through a strange language that occupies different dimensions.

You can, of course, have a lot of fun creating an alien language (and, in terms of worldbuilding, this obviously makes your world richer). But creating an entire language system from scratch is very difficult. To start with, it's better to suggest a flavor of another language. You can do this through experimenting with word order (think of Yoda), or differences in subtlety and slang.

## GETTING IT RIGHT

You'll probably find that writing dialogue is a tricky process that requires a lot of drafting and re-drafting. To get started, I recommend imagining a scene, as follows:

Let's imagine that a boy is trying to persuade his mother to let him go and watch a space race. It will be difficult and expensive, but he's been wanting to do it for ages. First of all, plot out the coordinates of the scene. Where is it taking place? What time of day? What room in the house? Where is the mother sitting or standing? And where is the boy?

Once you've got all that sorted out, then write a summary of the scene, without using any dialogue at all. For example:

"Yola enters the sitting room and sees his mother sitting with her VR headset on. He creeps up to her and taps her on the shoulder. She removes the VR set and they discuss the situation. Yola manages to persuade his mother that he is allowed to go to the race, but only if he promises to take his sister too."

Now imagine the same scene, but with Yola and his mother speaking. You could try writing a longer speech, in which Yola explains everything to his mother about why he wants to go to the race. You'll then understand him and his desires better. You could then give the mother a long speech, in which she outlines all the reasons she doesn't want him to go to the race and also why she wants him to take his sister. Here's an example:

**Yola:** "Mom, I really want to go because I love X-51 and Y-78, and they're not going to come here to race for years, and I've got enough coin in my account to go because I've been saving since my last birthday, and also I really want to be a racer and I think I can pick up some tricks from them, and also this girl I like is going and I want to impress her with my knowledge."

**Mom:** "Yola, you know I don't like you going to the racetrack. It's dirty and dangerous and there's lots of strange people there. I want you to spend more time with your sister, and I don't want you spending all your money on these frivolous expeditions. Why can't you be a doctor like your father?"

You'll have too much dialogue, now. If you have a big block like this, it's a big neon sign saying: "CUT ME, CUT ME." So, you'll need to trim it back. You can take out the unessential parts and just focus on what's important. And remember that very often, dialogue conceals other things and also that people say what they mean in other ways. Let's look at the scene again:

"When Yola entered the room, he saw his mother sitting slumped on the sofa with her VR headset on. It was flickering gently. Softly, he pressed her on the elbow and, with a sigh, she removed it.

'Dinner's soon,' she said, and placed the headset back in its port. She gazed at it a little too long. He wondered if she'd been looking at Earth again.

'I'll do the washing up,' said Yola. 'And I'll clean out the stables.'

His mother smiled, and ruffled his hair. 'Where's Suli?'

'In her room, I guess.'

His mother began to lift herself up out of her chair, and Yola thought that now was the time to ask, before she started worrying about his father again. 'So you know that thing I was telling you about . . . well, X-51's coming to town this weekend.'

'Who's that? Oh, your center racer.' A crease appeared on her forehead. 'We've got your aunt coming to visit. Her hospital sent her here specially to deal with the new colonists.'

'I'll clean the jets for a month.'

She paused by the door. He saw something flicker over her face. 'Suli will go with you?'

Yola didn't want her to. She was older than he was and didn't know anything about racing. She would find it really boring and would want to drag him back home early. But if that was the only way. . . ."

As you see can here, the reader can infer that there's a lot more going on behind what both characters are saying. This approach helps them become more involved in a story.

SO REMEMBER: KEEP IT SHORT, KEEP IT SIMPLE, KEEP IT LIVELY. AND YOU'LL HAVE A BLAST.

# LANGUAGE

**WHEN WRITING SPEECH,** you can use different techniques to create different effects. Some writers only like to use "said." Of course, sometimes people need to shout or whisper, but, in general, you're on pretty solid ground with "said."

Many writing manuals will tell you to avoid more specific words. I think this is a matter of opinion. If you want to write "she expectorated" (basically, she spat), then I give you full and free license to do so—you just have to make sure you're using the word in the right way and that it suits the style of your story. Other writers will use gesture: "Thanks!" she shrugged. This can be good for creating atmosphere and for deepening character. It's important, too, to remember that you can also write: "She was silent."

PICK UP A FEW BOOKS AND MAKE A LIST OF ALL THE
DIALOGUE TAGS YOU CAN FIND. THEN LIST BELOW THE ONES
YOU WANT TO USE IN YOUR OWN WRITING.

......................................................................................

......................................................................................

......................................................................................

......................................................................................

......................................................................................

......................................................................................

......................................................................................

......................................................................................

......................................................................................

......................................................................................

......................................................................................

......................................................................................

......................................................................................

......................................................................................

......................................................................................

# DIALOGUE EXAMPLE

**SAM:** YOUR DECK'S LOOKING A BIT MESSY . . .
I THINK YOU COULD USE A BIT MORE HELP.

**AMONA:** MY CREW CAN LOOK AFTER IT BY THEMSELVES,
THANK YOU VERY MUCH.

**SAM:** I . . . I, ER . . .

**AMONA:** NO THANK YOU.

**SAM:** POTATOES.

**AMONA:** I'M SORRY?

**SAM:** YOU'VE GOT SACKLOADS OF POTATOES. COME ON,
NOBODY LIKES PEELING POTATOES! I'LL DO IT, I PROMISE. JUST
TAKE ME WITH YOU.

## AMONA PAUSES, AND NODS, AND TURNS, ALLOWING SAM TO FOLLOW. . . .

○ Now work out what happens next, and continue the dialogue here!

# ARTIFICIAL INTELLIGENCE

**ARTIFICIAL INTELLIGENCE, OR AI, IS ALREADY EVERYWHERE.**
You probably have a smartphone and a laptop. You may even have a smart speaker in your house. Your television knows what you like. Maybe your fridge even orders snacks for you when you've run out of nuggets. (Excuse me for a second, I just need to . . . ah, wonderful, yes, thank you fridge.) Now then.

We have grown used to ease and convenience in our everyday lives. No more going down to the store to pick up some groceries for me, no sir. One click of a button and a package arrives at the house the very next day. But think of the consequences of that simple action. We don't, for example, see the robots at the packing factories, the complicated delivery algorithms, or the processes beneath the surface.

So what, you may be thinking? Why does it matter if YouTube feeds me videos I like? Or Siri records my voice? Or my birthday present arrives on time? Well, problems can arise when computational intelligence has an impact on real lives. What if that algorithm (see page 149) starts sending you toward damaging and dangerous videos? What if your voice is used for something you didn't even do or wanted? What if your package arriving on time means that more energy is used and more damaging gases are expelled into the atmosphere?

Then think about wider issues: if you can use an algorithm to predict and award exam results, then why not an algorithm that can make judgments in court cases? And then the problem arises: who makes the algorithm that decides a court case? And more frighteningly, perhaps, who programs the computer that drives our car, which then decides whether to save us or allow us to crash?

There are different forms of AI. We have already looked in detail at androids and robots. But there are also the intelligences of computers themselves; networked computers; avatars; and computer programs. The possibilities are both dizzying and endless. In Philip Reeve's Railhead series, artificial intelligences inhabit the data sea and appear as gods, interfering in human matters.

Many in sci-fi talk about the Singularity: a point at which machines will become super-intelligent and realize that they are more intelligent than humans. It is the stuff of nightmares. (My own hope is that technology usually ends up being not very good—and can always be switched off. If your laptop starts talking back to you, you know what to do.) Other ethical issues arise too: if an artificial intelligence becomes self-aware, then is it classed as human? And then, what does it mean to turn one off?

Imagine making a computer program to create a digital pet. What would happen as the pet grew and changed? Would you be able to develop a friendship with it? And what if, instead of a pet, you created a virtual person instead?

Think about a world in which everybody was protected by a massive company. And imagine if this world was run by a giant AI, which controlled everybody. Terrifying? Or comforting?

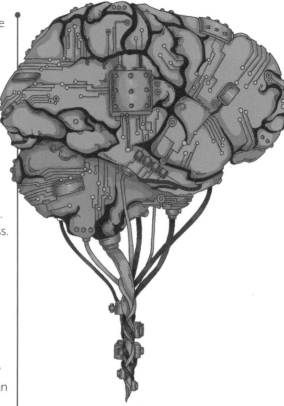

A CYBERBRAIN IS A NORMAL HUMAN BRAIN WITH ADDED ELECTRONIC COMPONENTS. IT COULD, POTENTIALLY, HAVE A DIRECT LINK TO THE INTERNET WITHOUT THE USE OF ANY DEVICES.

In *The Homework Machine* by Dan Gutman, Brenton, Sam, Judy, and Kelsey have a homework machine called Belch. Sounds like a dream, doesn't it? Well—watch out, as it soon starts creating more problems than it solves.

With artificial intelligence, it's good to start on a small scale. The following prompts will help you keep an eye out for those meddlesome algorithms.

# ARTIFICIAL INTELLIGENCE: WRITING PROMPTS

**1. BLIND DATE** A teenager receives a new phone with an AI organizer. It starts to try to organize the teenager's life. Write a scene in which the AI attempts to get the protagonist to go on a date with someone.

**2. SCIENTISTS ON THE RAMPAGE** A scientist transfers herself into a computer and runs amok. She starts by taking small revenges and progresses to larger ones. Write a first-person account of her time as an AI, before she gets unplugged.

**3. I AM A POET, BUT I DON'T KNOW IT** Write a five-verse poem from the point of view of a newly self-aware AI avatar. Use the following words: BIRD, GREEN, SHOUT, WANDER.

**4. TRAFFIC LIGHT TERROR** The local city center has been taken over by a malicious AI. Only a 15-year-old girl and her loyal friend can stop it. Describe a scene in which the girl and her friend plan their attempt to foil the AI.

**5. SELF-AWARENESS** An only child realizes that all his life he has been manipulated by an AI. Describe the scene when he realizes this.

## KEY WORDS

### MACHINE LEARNING

A computer system that can learn and improve without following exact instructions to do so.

**CLEVER THING**
In 2011, a computer played on the TV game show *Jeopardy*—and won.

# CHAPTER 5

# FORM AND PERSPECTIVE

SCI-FI SUITS LOTS OF DIFFERENT FORMS. SHORT STORIES, NOVELS, PLAYS, FILM SCRIPTS . . . HOW ABOUT A POEM? AND EACH HAS ITS OWN PROS AND CONS.

When you're starting out, I'd suggest doing a short story. You can work on a single idea—let's say, a robot raccoon—and then work it out fully. There are thousands of sci-fi short stories, and they're also a great place to start learning about the genre.

With the Internet, many writers can now publish their work online in the form of flash fiction—very, very short stories. A search online will reveal hundreds of sites where you can read people's work and contribute your own. With such short fiction, think very carefully about what you're doing and why. So, no backstory, not too many names, and focus on a single person.

A novel is a much more complex thing. You'll need to plan it carefully. This is the same with scripts and TV shows. Whatever form you choose, you'll have to think carefully about which point of view you choose.

There's a famous short story by Julio Cortazar called "Axolotl." In it, a man becomes obsessed with an axolotl. He goes to look at the axolotl every single day. Suddenly, the point of view changes, and you realize that he is the axolotl. That kind of thing can be really fun to do in sci-fi. But then who was telling us the story and from what point of view was it told?

## FIRST-PERSON

If you are using a first-person perspective (this is when the narrator is a character in the story, often the protagonist, and uses the pronouns I, us, me, or we), you need to think carefully about voice and knowledge. Worldbuilding can be harder to do from this point of view, but you can create an intriguing and compelling voice, as in Meg Rosoff's sci-fi-influenced *How I Live Now* (which was turned into a film with Saoirse Ronan) or Patrick Ness's Chaos Walking trilogy, where he switches between three equally engrossing first-person perspectives. However, most sci-fi will use the third person (when the narrator addresses the characters by name or he/she/they). Here you will have to think about whether to use the third-person omniscient, where the narrative voice knows everything about the story and its characters, or the third-person limited, where the voice is limited to what the character knows. Sci-fi lends itself nicely to the omniscient, which is particularly useful for backstory and exposition; but there is an extra emotional charge when you use the third-person limited. Although there is no law against what some call "head-hopping," where the writer tells you one person's thoughts before dipping into someone else's, many editors prefer a scene to be told through one person's perspective only. Here is an example of each:

## THIRD-PERSON OMNISCIENT

*In the star system Anthropo 67, there is a galaxy known as The Ear; in one of its farthest spirals, there lies the planetary system Co-By 124. And its main planet, the glittering red- and green-surfaced Yulitho, home to the glorious civilizations of Andor and Nethri, was only a few weeks away from a visit that would change the lives of its inhabitants forever. . . .*

## THIRD-PERSON LIMITED

*Joran searched the viewing screen, spiraling out from his house in the center of Andor, up through the gas clouds from where the Earth* *looked like a red and green tapestry. Yulitho, he thought. You are beautiful. Hanging here, like a jewel, in a planetary system where no other life breathes. He paused for a moment, taking in the view of the system. And then he saw a blinking dot at the edge of the screen, moving slowly. A battleship, he thought. It could only be one. He pressed a button to send the information to high command, and then took a sip of water.*

A strong perspective will help your narrative along. You could even experiment with the second person (you) or first-person plural (we). Imagine writing a story from the point of view of an all-powerful AI. . . .

# EXPERIMENTING WITH FORM

**ONE OF THE PROBLEMS WITH SCI-FI** is that there are, ultimately, only a handful of plots. (Remember, though, that it's what you do with them that counts.) It's all too easy to fall into a standard structure and form. And, partly, sci-fi is about breaking out of structures and forms.

Who's to say that you can't write an epic poem about the discovery of a new planet? Or a series of text messages, sent between planets, describing the love affair between a Blatovian Fungazoid and a four-legged Mathavan? Think about the many forms all around you: text messages, social media messages and feeds, websites, journals, blogs, essays, diaries, logs, letters . . . the more you play about with these ideas, the more interesting places you will rocket off to. Jay Kristoff and Amie Kaufman do this well in *Illuminae* with emails, medical reports, interviews, and more.

Think about all the fun things you could do with your text. Even experimenting with fonts can make great effects.

If you play around with size as well, you can find a way of showing different languages or **BIG NOISES.**

You could write a story in a circle, so the reader has to turn the page around. You could punch a hole in the paper so that you can see through to another layer underneath.

You could type your story in mirror writing, or in code. You could write it on cards and then randomly select them to create another story. You could build a hypertext story on a computer, with links taking the reader to different outcomes. You could find a buddy and write one section of a story after another.

You can also spice up your story with bits of other forms. Frank Herbert's *Dune*, for example, breaks up the main narrative with excerpts from imagined history books and dictionaries, all of which help to create the sense of a fully formed universe.

Sci-fi is also a genre that can be imitated in a comical way very easily. There are lots of funny books around—*Warcross* by Marie Lu is hilarious, as is *Landscape with Invisible Hand* by M.T. Anderson, in which planet Earth is taken over by a species that resembles coffee tables. Some people even start to scuttle on their backs, palms down, just to fit in.

Think about other genres—detective thrillers, mysteries, horror—and then think about how you could use them for sci-fi. How about a detective novel set on Mars?

And there are many other things you can do. One of the books I remember enjoying most as an early adolescent was *Alice in Quantumland* by Robert Gilmore. It used the story of *Alice in Wonderland* to explain the realities of quantum physics. And I can still remember a lot of it, thirty years later.

Remember: boundaries of form are there to be broken. With a giant, pulsing laser blast.

≫

WHY NOT TURN YOUR FAVORITE, OR LEAST FAVORITE, FOOD INTO AN ALIEN? PHILIP REEVE'S *CAKES IN SPACE* HAS SENTIENT, EVIL KILLER CAKES, AND JEFF VANDERMEER'S *FINCH* HAS A PLANET RUN BY MUSHROOMS.

# FORM: WRITING PROMPTS

**1. OH, WHAT CAN AIL THEE, DROID AT ARMS?** Choose a ballad (see page 158), or a poem you like. Now use the structure of the ballad or poem, but set it in a sci-fi world.

**2. IN A FLASH** Write a flash fiction based on one of the following scenarios: time stops; a dinosaur wakes up; a massive tentacle is found on top of a church.

**3. GO, GO GEOMETRY** Choose a shape (circle, square, etc.) and then base a story on the form of the shape. Write it out in that form (e.g., draw a triangle and then write your story about a triangle within the shape itself). Perhaps the shape will inspire a new spaceship design.

**4. TRY IT THREE WAYS** Use this scenario: a man walks into a café, and finds a robot behind the counter and an alien at one of the tables. Write a diary account of the situation from the perspective of each one: the man, the robot, and the alien.

**5. EXCEED YOUR LIMITATIONS** Describe a visit to an alien temple. Apply one of the following limitations:
- Don't use words containing the letter "e."
- Only use words of one syllable.
- Write in a foreign language.

FORM AND PERSPECTIVE

**PANDEMIC**

Jennifer L. Holm's novel, *The Lion of Mars*, deals with a virus that affects only adults on the US colony on Mars. Though written before the COVID-19 pandemic, it does give a good example of how real-life can inspire your sci-fi story.

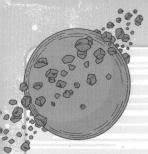

# CHAPTER 6

# ENDINGS

SO, YOU'VE MADE IT TO THE END. WE ALL ENJOY A GOOD ENDING: THE SATISFACTION OF SEEING THE STORY REACH ITS CONCLUSION. YOUR ROBOT HAS FOUND HIS LONG-LOST MAKER. YOUR WORLD HAS BEEN SAVED. YOUR GIANT RABBIT HAS FOUND A PLACE TO LIVE WHERE HE WILL NO LONGER HAVE TO LOOK FOR CARROTS EVER AGAIN. (WELL, MAYBE NOT THAT LAST ONE.)

**AS ARISTOTLE WROTE** in *Poetics*: an ending "naturally follows some other thing . . . but has nothing following it." In other words, every action in your plot has a consequence, and the ending is the final consequence.

Your reader has been invested in so many things during the course of your work. Reading a work of fiction takes time (and gives the illusion of time passing too): hence the desire for a good ending. Your reader has spent a long time with your writing. They have marvelled at the setting. They've enjoyed meeting the characters. They've wanted to know what will happen to them.

And now they want to know how it all ends. In the right sort of way. What goes up, must come down.

And we all know what a good ending feels like. We put down the book, knowing that every bit of the story has been neatly tied up and also, perhaps, made a little more aware of the messiness of life itself.

## THE NATURE OF THE BEAST

Due to the nature of the genre, the endings in sci-fi tend to be familiar. The Earth is saved, the aliens are defeated, the meteorite is deflected, the plague is cured, and so on. Any story will have a movement toward an ending—that's partly why stories work, because the reader expects to be led along toward a definite moment.

In a fairy story, we expect the third daughter to win out where the first two have failed; we expect Gretel to push the witch into the oven (see image on the left illustrating the ending of *Hansel and Gretel*); we expect Gerda to find Kay in *The Snow Queen*. And part of the fun with endings is that you can play around with those expectations.

For example, you could be leading us along to thinking that everything is going to be destroyed—and then, kapow! At the very last minute, everything changes and the world is saved. Remember, if you do this, it still has to work within the mechanics of the plot. But try to avoid using a *deus ex machina* (a term from Greek drama where a god would descend onto the stage and solve everything)—in other words, where something unexpected happens out of nowhere and everything is resolved.

## A STING IN THE TAIL

Sci-fi endings can often have a "sting in the tail," where everything you thought you knew is upended. Again, it's important for your ending to be part of the logic of the plot: you can't just suddenly turn round and say, "And it turned out that he was a butterfly AI avatar all along" or even "And the cat did it!"

You have to lead the reader along, hinting at possibilities through the action of the plot, then pull the rug out from underneath them. Orson Scott Card's *Ender's Game* has a brilliant twist that resonates throughout the book. What is it, you ask? Well, spoiler alert: I won't tell you. But I CAN tell you (since it's entered into popular culture) about George Orwell's *Nineteen Eighty-Four*. If you don't know the story, it's about a world in which communism has taken over.

Britain is now known as Airstrip One, and there are two classes: party members (the inner and outer) and proletarians (the working class). Everybody is watched, all the time, through a screen installed in their houses. Winston, a party member, becomes increasingly concerned about what he sees and hears. Toward the end, he believes he has penetrated into the heart of the oppressive government: only to become aware of how pointless his attempts at resistance are. It's a terrifyingly powerful work.

## THE UNCERTAINTY PRINCIPLE

We like fiction since it imposes order onto things. But another way of ending your work is with an event that leaves things a little uncertain. This is a little closer to what life is really like, and it can be equally satisfying as an ending in which there are no loose ends.

Sci-fi quite often deals straightforwardly with Good versus Evil. But in a more complex work, we could think about how those can be a matter of perspective. In a war, who is necessarily right? An ambiguous ending might leave us with a feeling that the main character could perhaps have taken a different route, or that the consequences of the plot might lead somewhere unintended. Perhaps your protagonist was wrong in believing that the Kulhairan Emperor was the right person to lead the universe after all.

# THE END OF THE UNIVERSE

**ONE OF THE MOST DIFFICULT AND MIND-BOGGLING IDEAS TO GRASP** is that, eventually, the universe will come to an end. Not in our lifetimes, or in the lifetimes of our descendants, but so far into the future that it seems unimaginable.

Entropy means that everything tends toward chaos: once energy has been expended, there's no way of making it come back again. Pretty gloomy, huh? It's unsurprising, then, that lots of sci-fi is set against a backdrop of the end of, well, literally everything. Plenty of sci-fi has the world threatened through one form or another, whether it's a dying sun or a meteorite strike or an alien invasion. And there is a thriving sub-genre set at the actual end of the universe itself. For example, Charles Sheffield's *Between the Strokes of Night* is partly set right at the end of the universe, before the Big Crunch happens. It deals with human colonies so far into the future that they have all but forgotten their Earth-origins. Strange, massive entities exist in between galaxies: one of the characters witnesses the actual end of the universe itself. Mind-boggling stuff. Similarly, the universe is approaching a Big Crunch in *Tau Zero* by Poul Anderson—in this novel, the crew manage a more hopeful ending (without giving too much away, of course).

And, to end on a lighter note, Douglas Adams plays with many of the sci-fi tropes about the end of the universe in *The Restaurant at the End of the Universe*, in which the restaurant of the title exists in a time bubble at the place where the universe ends—and it offers diners a brilliant view of it all. What better than to kick back with a nice meal when apocalypse threatens?

It doesn't have to be all doom, gloom, and horrible nano-robots turning everything into gray goo, you see. The great thing about imagining everything collapsing entirely is that it also allows us to envisage situations in which it doesn't. Could you transfer the entire universe through a portal into a parallel world? Or is there some other way of doing it? Well? I'm waiting. . . . Yes, that's right. Only YOU can save the universe. And you have 24 hours to do it. . . .

# ENDING: WRITING PROMPTS

**1. CAPTAIN'S LOG** Write the captain's log for a ship whose mission it is to find the beginning of the end of the universe.

**2. DIFFERENT DISASTERS** Write down three different ways the universe might end. Be as imaginative as you can. For instance: a giant space bat eats everything.

**3. GODLIKE POWERS** Write an account, from a god's point of view, of what the end of the universe would be like.

**4. MYSTERIOUS SURVIVAL** One spaceship mysteriously survives the end of everything. Write a first-person account of the day after the end.

**5. BEGIN AGAIN** A spaceship has finally reached what the crew think is the end of the universe—only for it to reappear back where it started. Describe the moment the navigator realizes that this has happened.

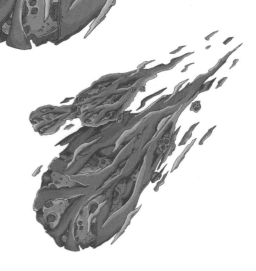

**KEY WORD**
APOCALYPSE
A total catastrophe or even
the end of the world.

**KEY WORD**
ENTROPY
The way the universe tends
toward disorder.

ENDINGS

**DON'T WORRY**

Scientists think the earliest possible time the universe could end will be about 22 billion years in the future. So, you'll still need to hand your homework in.

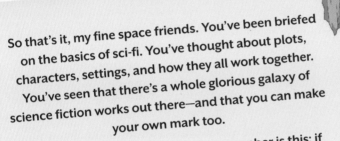

So that's it, my fine space friends. You've been briefed on the basics of sci-fi. You've thought about plots, characters, settings, and how they all work together. You've seen that there's a whole glorious galaxy of science fiction works out there—and that you can make your own mark too.

Perhaps the most crucial point to remember is this: if you find yourself writing something that feels like it's been written before, then think again. Look at things from new angles, new perspectives. Keep yourself informed of what's happening in the news. Has a scientist unlocked a new gene? Has a technological company released a new kind of robot? What will the consequences be? How might it affect real people, now? And how might it affect real people in the future? Sci-fi can predict the future, but it can also act as a warning.

And most of all: remember that writing sci-fi can be fun too. Now go forth, my galactic friends, and scribble away till the world ends.

GRAB A BITE TO EAT AT THE RESTAURANT AT THE END OF THE UNIVERSE—OR JUST READ DOUGLAS ADAMS' HILARIOUS NOVEL *THE RESTAURANT AT THE END OF THE UNIVERSE* INSTEAD.

# READING LIST

READING MAKES YOU A BETTER WRITER. YOU'LL LEARN NEW WRITING STYLES AND VOCABULARY, AND YOU MIGHT EVEN GET AN IDEA FOR YOUR OWN BOOK. USE THE BELOW LIST AS YOUR PERSONAL READING LIST AND CHECK OFF EACH BOOK AFTER YOU HAVE READ IT.

- ☐ *A Blade So Black* by L. L. McKinney
- ☐ *Alice in Quantumland* by Robert Gilmore
- ☐ *A Wrinkle in Time* by Madeleine L'Engle
- ☐ *Bloom* by Kenneth Oppel
- ☐ *Brave New World* by Aldous Huxley
- ☐ *Cakes in Space* by Philip Reeve
- ☐ *Chaos Walking trilogy* by Patrick Ness
- ☐ *Cinder* by Marissa Meyer
- ☐ *Clockwork Planet* by Yuu Kamiya and Tsubaki Himana
- ☐ *Dragon Pearl* by Yoon Ha Lee
- ☐ *Dreambender* by Ronald Kidd
- ☐ *Dune* by Frank Herbert
- ☐ *Dune: The Butlerian Jihad* by Brian Herbert and Kevin J Anderson
- ☐ *Edge of Extinction: The Ark Plan* by Laura Martin
- ☐ *Ender's Game* by Orson Scott Card
- ☐ *Everfair* by Nisi Shawl
- ☐ *Frankenstein* by Mary Shelley
- ☐ *Frankenstein in Baghdad* by Ahmed Saadawi
- ☐ *From the Earth to the Moon* by Jules Verne
- ☐ *George's Secret Key to the Universe* by Lucy and Stephen Hawking
- ☐ *Girl Gone Viral* by Arvin Ahmadi
- ☐ *Gulliver's Travels* by Jonathan Swift
- ☐ *Ikenga* by Nnedi Okorafor
- ☐ *Illuminae* by Jay Kristoff and Amie Kaufman
- ☐ *Incarceron* by Catherine Fisher
- ☐ *I, Robot* by Isaac Asimov
- ☐ *Jinks & O'Hare, Funfair Repair* by Philip Reeve
- ☐ *Landscape with Invisible Hand* by M.T. Anderson
- ☐ *Little Brother* by Cory Doctorow

- ☐ *Maggot Moon* by Sally Gardner
- ☐ *Mars Evacuees* by Sophia McDougall
- ☐ *Mount Misery* by Angelo Peluso
- ☐ *Neuromancer* by William Gibson
- ☐ *Nineteen Eighty-Four* by George Orwell
- ☐ *Railhead* by Philip Reeve
- ☐ *Ready Player One* by Ernest Cline
- ☐ *Root Magic* by Eden Royce
- ☐ *Skyward series* by Brandon Sanderson
- ☐ *Snow Crash* by Neal Stephenson
- ☐ *Starman's Quest* by Robert Silverberg
- ☐ *Stories of Your Life and Others* by Ted Chiang
- ☐ *Tau Zero* by Poul Anderson
- ☐ *The Changes Trilogy* by Peter Dickinson
- ☐ *The Culture series* by Iain M. Banks
- ☐ *The Dark Lord of Derkholm* by Diana Wynne Jones
- ☐ *The Dispossessed* by Ursula K. Le Guin
- ☐ *The Drowned World* by J.G. Ballard
- ☐ *The Giver* by Lois Lowry
- ☐ *The Hitchhiker's Guide to the Galaxy* by Douglas Adams
- ☐ *The Homework Machine* by Dan Gutman
- ☐ *The Hunger Games* by Suzanne Collins
- ☐ *The Iron Man* by Ted Hughes
- ☐ *The Jupiter Pirates: Hunt for the Hydra* by Jason Fry
- ☐ *The Larklight trilogy* by Philip Reeve
- ☐ *The Last Human* by Lee Bacon
- ☐ *The Last Kids on Earth* by Max Brallier
- ☐ *The Lathe of Heaven* by Ursula K. Le Guin
- ☐ *The Left Hand of Darkness* by Ursula K. Le Guin
- ☐ *The Lifecycle of Software Objects* by Ted Chiang

- ☐ *The Line* by Teri Hall
- ☐ *The Long Earth* by Terry Pratchett and Stephen Baxter
- ☐ *The Man in the High Castle* by Philip K. Dick
- ☐ *The Many Worlds of Albie Bright* by Christopher Edge
- ☐ *The Mathenauts* by Norman Kagan
- ☐ *The Plot Against America* by Philip Roth
- ☐ *The Railway Children* by E. Nesbit
- ☐ *The Restaurant at the End of the Universe* by Douglas Adams
- ☐ *The Search for Wondla* by Tony DiTerlizzi
- ☐ *The Sin Eater's Daughter* by Melissa Salisbury
- ☐ *The Star-Touched Queen* by Roshani Chokshi
- ☐ *The Story of the Amulet* by E. Nesbit
- ☐ *The Time Machine* by H. G. Wells
- ☐ *The Trial* by Franz Kafka
- ☐ *The True Meaning of Smekday* by Adam Rex
- ☐ *The Unseen World* by Liz Moore
- ☐ *The War of the Worlds* by H. G. Wells
- ☐ *Trapped in a Video Game* by Dustin Brady
- ☐ *Trillions* by Nicholas Fisk
- ☐ *Utopia* by Thomas More
- ☐ *Warcross* by Marie Lu

## SHORT STORIES

- ☐ *"A Sound of Thunder"* by Ray Bradbury
- ☐ *"The Machine Stops"* by E. M. Forster

## WRITING BOOKS

- ☐ *Poetics* by Aristotle
- ☐ *The Hero with a Thousand Faces* by Joseph Campbell
- ☐ *The Seven Basic Plots* by Christopher Booker

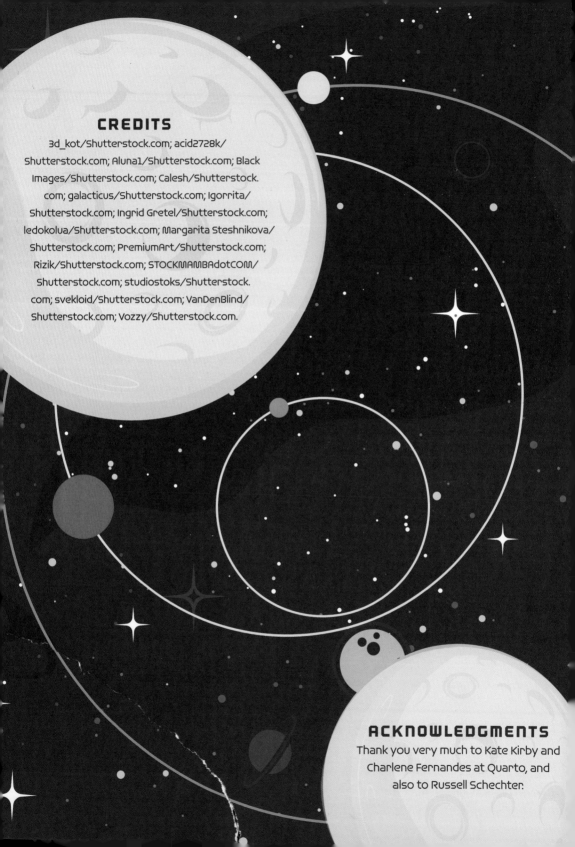

## CREDITS

3d_kot/Shutterstock.com; acid2728k/
Shutterstock.com; Aluna1/Shutterstock.com; Black
Images/Shutterstock.com; Calesh/Shutterstock.
com; galacticus/Shutterstock.com; Igorrita/
Shutterstock.com; Ingrid Gretel/Shutterstock.com;
ledokolua/Shutterstock.com; Margarita Steshnikova/
Shutterstock.com; PremiumArt/Shutterstock.com;
Rizik/Shutterstock.com; STOCKMAMBAdotCOM/
Shutterstock.com; studiostoks/Shutterstock.
com; svekloid/Shutterstock.com; VanDenBlind/
Shutterstock.com; Vozzy/Shutterstock.com.

## ACKNOWLEDGMENTS

Thank you very much to Kate Kirby and
Charlene Fernandes at Quarto, and
also to Russell Schechter.